Vegetable Gardener's Mastery [10 Books In 1]: Unlock the Power of the G.R.O.W System for High-Yield Organic Gardening. Proven Techniques & Expert Secrets. Your Essential Guide for Bountiful Harvests

1st Edition

ISBN: 978-1-916825-01-7

Sites:
Company: mindsparkpressltd.com
Benjamin Greenfield: benjamingreenfieldbooks.com

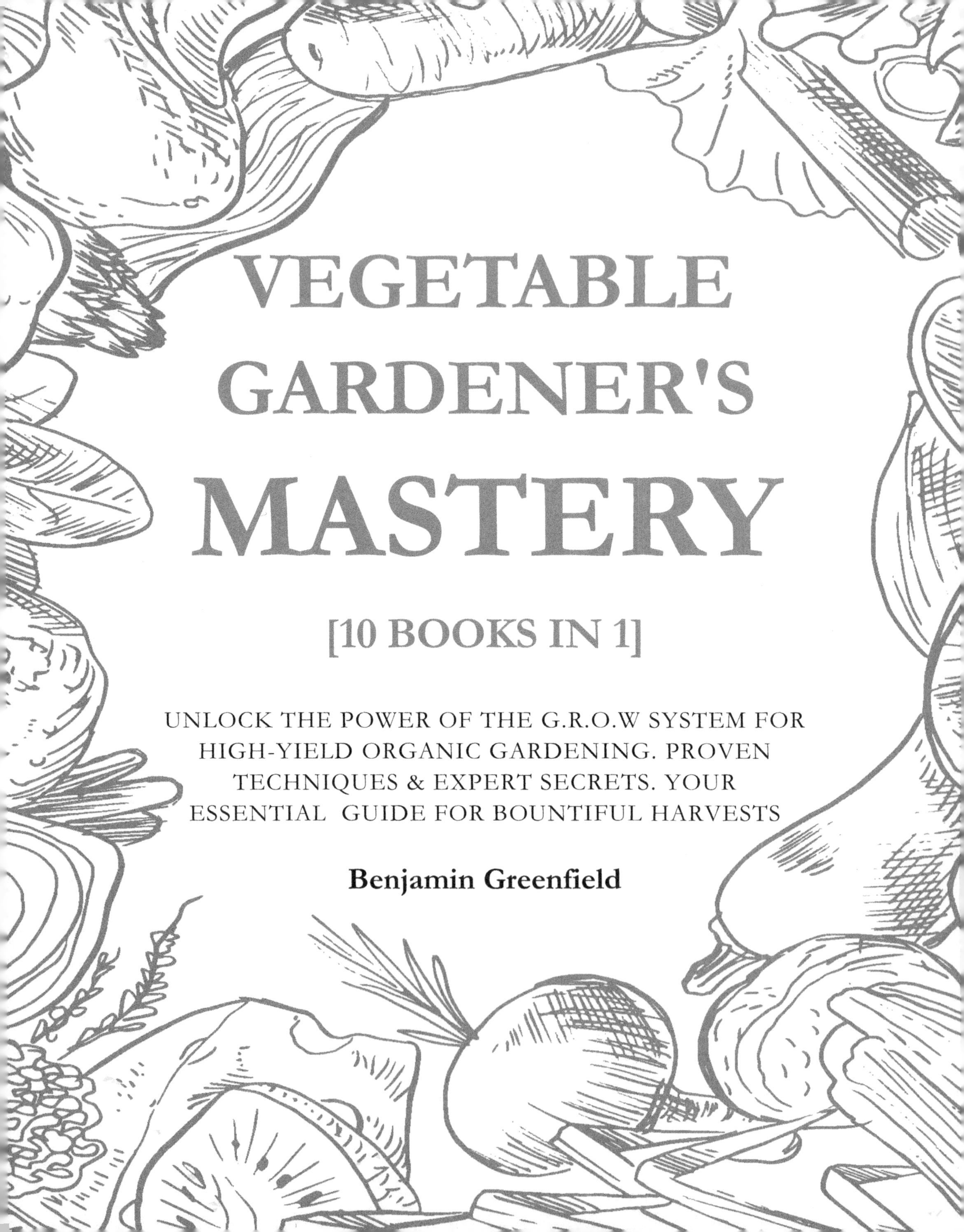

VEGETABLE GARDENER'S MASTERY

[10 BOOKS IN 1]

UNLOCK THE POWER OF THE G.R.O.W SYSTEM FOR HIGH-YIELD ORGANIC GARDENING. PROVEN TECHNIQUES & EXPERT SECRETS. YOUR ESSENTIAL GUIDE FOR BOUNTIFUL HARVESTS

Benjamin Greenfield

PREFACTION

"As I held this book, "Vegetable Gardener's Mastery," in my hands, I found myself immersed in a captivating journey through the world of gardening and sustainable living. From the very first page, the words leapt out at me, weaving a tapestry of knowledge and inspiration that spoke directly to my passion for cultivating the earth and reaping its bountiful rewards. I was about to embark on a remarkable expedition, led by the expertise and dedication of Benjamin Greenfield, the author of this enlightening work.

In a world where our connection with nature is often overshadowed by the demands of modern life, "Vegetable Gardener's Mastery" shines as a beacon of guidance and empowerment. Through the pages of this remarkable book, Benjamin Greenfield adeptly navigates the complexities of gardening, offering insights that resonate with both beginners and seasoned gardeners. With each chapter, I felt a growing sense of enthusiasm and confidence, as if I were being gently ushered toward a more sustainable and harmonious way of life.

Benjamin Greenfield's words are infused with both passion and expertise, creating a space where readers can delve into the art and science of gardening with renewed vigor. As the author skillfully interweaves horticultural wisdom, ecological consciousness, and practical tips, I found myself captivated by the transformative potential of these sustainable practices.

Throughout "Vegetable Gardener's Mastery," Benjamin Greenfield takes us on a journey through the joys and challenges of cultivating the land, providing us with invaluable tools and heartfelt encouragement. With each turn of the page, I felt a deepening connection to the earth and a sense of purpose in tending to its fertile soil. From preparing the ground to nurturing seedlings, this book leaves no stone unturned in its quest to empower us with the skills and knowledge to create thriving gardens and sustainable landscapes.

As I reached the final chapters, a sense of gratitude washed over me for the transformative experience I had just encountered. "Vegetable Gardener's Mastery" is a testament to the profound impact that our connection with the land can have on our lives and the environment. It is a gift to anyone seeking to harness the power of gardening to nourish the body, mind, and soul, while fostering a deeper relationship with the natural world.

To all who embark on this journey with "Vegetable Gardener's Mastery" in hand, I encourage you to embrace the teachings within these pages with an open heart and a willingness to cultivate not only your garden but also a profound connection with the earth. Let Benjamin Greenfield's words be your guiding light as you master the art of sustainable gardening. May this book inspire growth, harmony, and abundance in both your garden and your life."

Rachel Roberts

TABLE OF CONTENTS

To all those who embark on the journey of sustainable gardening and holistic cultivation. May this book be a guiding light on your path to mastering the art of cultivating the earth, nurturing thriving gardens, and embracing the profound connection between nature and well-being. Your commitment to sustainable living inspires us to continue sharing the power of eco-conscious practices and their transformative potential. May you find fulfillment, harmony, and a deeper bond with the natural world through this exploration of mindful gardening.

With heartfelt gratitude,

Benjamin Greenfield

Introduction

In today's hectic world to engage in activities that connect us with nature and give us a sense of achievement. One such activity is growing our vegetables, which positively affects our physical wellbeing, mental clarity, and overall sense of purpose. The cultivation of vegetables has a history that spans across countries and generations. Humans have been cultivating vegetables for various reasons, including consumption, medicinal purposes, and aesthetic appeal, for centuries.

The G.R.O.W. System stands for;

- **G -** Good Soil Management Practices
- **R -** Responsible Water Usage
- **O -** Organic Pest and Disease Control
- **W -** Wise Crop Selection and Rotation

This system provides a framework for successful organic gardening by emphasizing the importance of proper soil management, efficient water utilization organic pest and disease prevention methods, as well as careful crop selection and rotation.

Health Benefits and Self-Sufficiency

Growing our vegetables goes beyond being a pleasurable hobby; it also offers numerous health benefits and enhances our overall quality of life. Consuming vegetables that are freshly grown from sources can potentially help in preventing or delaying the onset of chronic diseases, like cancer and heart conditions. Gardening is an activity that not only brings joy, but also has the potential to alleviate stress and improve our mental wellbeing.

This book offers advice, detailed instructions, and a strong focus on responsible practices, making it an invaluable resource for those who want to try their hand at growing vegetables. Lets delve into why its important to grow your vegetables the benefits it brings and how you can make the most of them.

Environmental Consciousness

Cultivating our vegetables allows us to become more self-sufficient and environmentally conscious. By reducing our reliance on food services through home gardening, we not only decrease our carbon footprint but also contribute positively towards the overall food system. Embracing farming techniques like composting and natural pest management helps us protect the environment while promoting biodiversity.

Nutritious Meals and Cost Savings

Secondly when it comes to health and nutrition nothing compares to vegetables. By growing our produce we ensure that our families have access to nutritious meals. It's a win win situation as it encourages better eating habits while nurturing our well being. Gardening also provides opportunities for exercise in the air and fosters a connection with nature – both of which are incredibly beneficial for physical and mental health.

Lastly, one cannot overlook the advantages of producing your own vegetables. Growing your veggies can significantly cut down on grocery bills, allowing you to save money in the long run.

In summary gardening offers a multitude of advantages – from fulfillment, to consciousness and improved health – all while providing us with delicious homegrown produce that nourishes both body and soul.
With the increasing cost of purchasing produce maintaining a kept garden can be a great way to save money. By investing in seeds and basic gardening tools, you can enjoy a plentiful harvest year after year, ensuring a supply of nutritious food.

Water Conservation

Another advantage of gardening is its impact on water conservation. In a society where water scarcity is becoming more prevalent practicing watering techniques like mulching, drip irrigation and rainwater collection allows us to save water without compromising the health or yield of our plants. Additionally reducing packaging and transportation in the process helps minimize waste and carbon emissions.

Community and Camaraderie

Furthermore engaging in vegetable cultivation creates a sense of belonging within a community. Connecting with gardening enthusiasts allows for conversations, exchange of ideas, and knowledge sharing. This camaraderie enhances the joy and benefits derived from gardening.

This vegetable growing guide serves as a valuable resource for aspiring gardeners. It provides practical and foolproof advice, emphasizing eco-friendly practices like composting, natural pest control, and water conservation. By adopting these approaches, gardeners not only contribute to the well-being of the planet but also enhance the ecological balance in their own gardens.

The book notable for its valuable guidance, detailed instructions, and emphasis on
sustainable practices. It encourages readers to explore gardening methods that not only benefit the environment but also lead to a sustainable lifestyle with reduced grocery expenses. The book presents information in various formats, such as blog posts, videos, and vibrant communities on platforms like Facebook, catering to different reading preferences. It fosters a sense of camaraderie and solidarity among novice gardeners, providing opportunities for sharing information and mentorship through forums, local gardening clubs, or organized events.

Overall, this book is an invaluable tool for cultivating vegetables, equipping readers for success right from their very first crop planting. By following the G.R.O.W. System and engaging in responsible practices, readers can enjoy a bountiful harvest while promoting a sustainable and eco-conscious lifestyle.

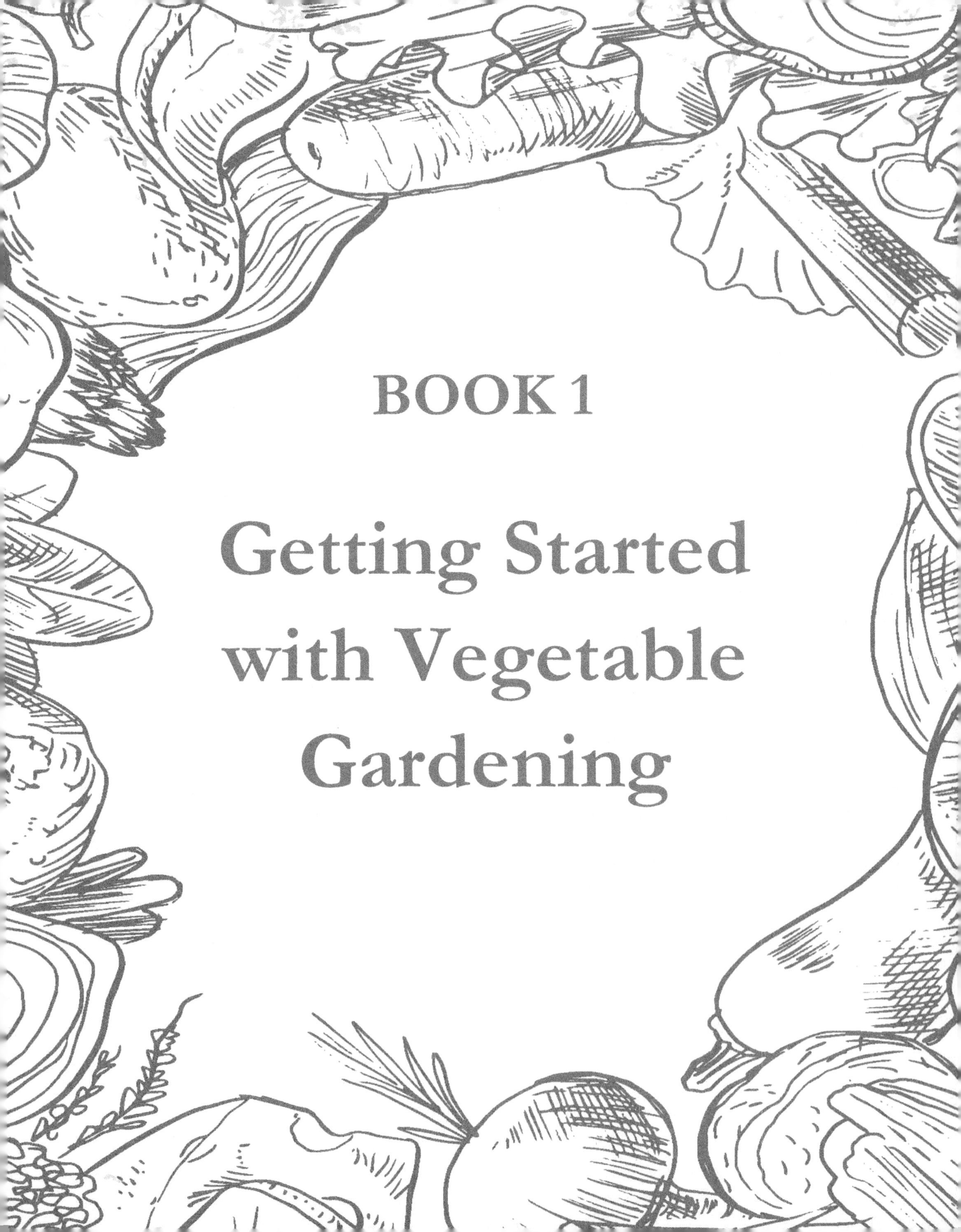

BOOK 1

Getting Started with Vegetable Gardening

Book 1: Getting Started with Vegetable Gardening

Introduction

Renowned gardening expert Benjamin Greenfield devised a system known as the G.R.O.W. Technique, which offers gardeners a comprehensive plan to maximize their harvests. This innovative strategy combines four elements— soil management practices (G), responsible water usage (R), organic methods for pest and disease control (O), and intelligent selection and rotation of crops (W)—to enhance gardening outcomes while adhering to an organic, eco-friendly approach.

- **(G) Good Soil Management Practices**
  Let's delve into the pillar Good Soil Management Practices (G). The soil serves as the cornerstone for any garden. Factors such as plant growth, nutrient availability, and overall soil health can all be optimized through soil management techniques. This involves steps like enriching the soil with matter such as compost or aged manure, along with efforts to improve its structure and drainage capabilities. By investing time and effort into establishing and maintaining the soil, you provide your plants with an environment that stimulates their growth and productivity.

- **(R) Responsible Water Usage**
  Next, it's important to be mindful of water usage for long-term sustainability. Efficient water management is an aspect of the G.R.O.W. System focusing on practices like mulching, drip irrigation, and rainwater collection. These methods help maximize water availability for plants while minimizing waste. It's crucial to avoid overwatering as it can lead to root rot and other plant diseases. By implementing water conservation measures, we can prevent these issues while still providing hydration for our crops.

- **(O) Organic Methods for Pest and Disease Control**
  In farming, using eco-friendly approaches to control pests and diseases is at the core of the G.R.O.W. System. Instead of relying on chemicals, we prioritize natural remedies for disease and pest control. Companion planting, attracting beneficial insects, utilizing organic or natural pesticides, and employing biological controls are some examples of these methods. Establishing a balanced ecology and implementing insect management techniques are effective ways to protect our plants without compromising the health of our environment.

- **(W) Wise Crop Selection and Rotation**
  To optimize yields while minimizing the spread of pests and diseases, the "Wise Crop Selection and Rotation" component of the G.R.O.W. System emphasizes planning when choosing which crops to cultivate. Considering factors such as crop compatibility, nutritional requirements, and disease susceptibility plays a role in this strategy. By cultivating a diverse range of crops and considering these factors, we can promote healthy growth while reducing risks associated with pests and diseases. Crop rotation and selective planting can enhance soil fertility, disrupt pest and disease cycles, and address various plant health issues.

Benjamin Greenfield's G.R.O.W. System provides a solid foundation for organic farming. By implementing Good Soil Management Practices, Responsible Water Usage, Organic Pest and Disease Control, and Wise Crop Selection and Rotation, gardeners can optimize productivity while upholding organic and sustainable principles. Prioritizing soil health, water efficiency, natural pest control methods, and thoughtful crop selection allows for a garden that yields nutrient-rich food while minimizing environmental impact. Embracing the G.R.O.W. System not only ensures plant protection but also contributes to a more balanced ecosystem and the overall well-being of our planet. With this framework as your guide, you'll embark on your gardening journey with confidence and achieve impressive outcomes.

Importance of Planning and Choosing the Right Location for Your

A successful and growing vegetable garden is built on careful planning and the selection of the ideal site. An attractive landscape and greater efficiency are guaranteed by careful design. Let's talk about the value of planning and the important factors to take into account when deciding where to put your garden.

1. **Sunlight Exposure**: Photosynthesis and the general growth and development of plants depend on sunlight. Consider the location's exposure to sunlight while designing your garden. The majority of vegetable plants need at least 6 to 8 hours a day of direct sunshine. To gauge how much sunshine the region gets, keep an eye on it throughout the day. Avoid places that may be shadowed by large trees, constructions, or other objects that might impede plant development and choose for a position that receives enough of sunshine.

2. **Soil Drainage**: For your plants to be healthy, the soil must drain properly. Check the soil drainage in the desired site before planting. Avoid regions with high clay soils that hold moisture or those that are prone to standing water. Look for soil with good drainage, which enables extra water to run out while yet holding in adequate moisture for the plants.

3. **Proximity to Water Sources**: Vegetable planting requires access to a dependable water supply. Consider the closeness of a water supply, such as a hose, rain barrel, or irrigation system, while designing your garden. Choosing a location close to a water supply makes watering easier and more effective, reducing the risk of under- or overwatering your plants. Additionally, it's crucial to make sure that the garden receives enough water coverage and pressure.

4. **Optimal Plant Growth**: Proper planning and site selection lead to optimum plant development. You can encourage plant growth by giving ample sunshine, well-drained soil, and easy access to water. As a consequence, the plants are healthier, with stronger root systems, vivid foliage, and copious harvests.

5. **Efficiency and Accessibility**: Planning your garden enables you to maximize accessibility and efficiency. Ensure your garden is practical in terms of its layout and design. Create walkways and bed configurations that are simple to access for planting, upkeep, and harvesting. You may enjoy and handle gardening duties better by effectively planning your garden to save time and effort.

6. **Aesthetics and Enjoyment**: Choosing the right location and planning your garden also contribute to its overall aesthetics and your enjoyment of the space. A well-designed garden enhances the visual appeal of your outdoor area, creating a pleasant and inviting environment. Incorporate elements like raised beds, trellises, and pathways to create a visually appealing and organized garden. A beautiful garden not only adds value to your property but also provides a peaceful and enjoyable space for relaxation and recreation.

Ensuring your vegetable garden is productive and gratifying requires careful planning and selecting the ideal area. Planning effectively maximizes plant growth, boosts productivity, and improves your garden's overall beauty. You may establish the conditions for a growing and aesthetically pleasing garden by providing your plants with a comfortable atmosphere and adding useful design elements. If you take the time to prepare and make informed decisions, you will have many years of successful and rewarding vegetable gardening.

Assessing Soil Quality and Implementing Good Soil Management Practices (G) For Optimal Plant Growth

Hence a general soil makeup that benefits most varieties is usually perfect.

1. **Importance of Soil Health**: Plant development and production are directly influenced by soil quality. A habitat that is suitable for beneficial soil organisms, balanced supply of nutrients, sufficient drainage, and appropriate aeration are all characteristics of healthy soil. It enables access to vital nutrients, promotes the growth of roots, and promotes plant vitality all around. By giving soil health the attention, it deserves, you create the conditions for resilient plants that can endure pests, diseases, and environmental pressures.

2. **Assessing Soil Quality**: By evaluating the soil's quality, one may ascertain the state of the soil and spot any imbalances or shortages that can hinder plant development. Several methods can be used to assess soil quality:

   - **Soil Testing**: Conduct a soil test to determine the nutrient content and pH level of your soil. A soil test report provides valuable information on the soil's fertility status and helps you adjust nutrient levels accordingly.

- **Texture Assessment**: Feel the earth between your fingertips to examine its texture. Clay soils feel sticky and compact, while sandy soils feel grittier. Loamy soils have a crumbly texture and are perfect for plant development since they have a mix of sand, silt, and clay.
- **Observation of Plant Growth**: Evaluate the growth and performance of plants in your garden. Poor plant growth, stunted development, or nutrient deficiency symptoms can indicate soil issues.

3. **Improving Soil Fertility and Structure**: Once you have assessed soil quality, implementing Good Soil Management Practices (GSMP)can help improve soil fertility and structure. Here are practical techniques to enhance soil health:

   - **Composting**: Composting is the process of converting organic waste, such as food scraps, yard clippings, and plant remnants, into nutrient-rich compost. Compost increases soil structure, improves moisture retention, and provides nutrients.
   - **Adding Organic Matter**: Add organic material to the soil, such as well-rotted compost, old manure, or leaf mulch. Improved soil structure, increased nutrient availability, improved water-holding capacity, and promoted beneficial microbial activity are all benefits of organic matter.
   - **Balancing pH Levels**: The availability of nutrients to plants depends on soil pH. Check the pH of your soil, and make any required adjustments. In alkaline soils, sulfur or organic matter may drop pH, while adding lime can increase pH in acidic soils.
   - **Mulching**: Apply organic mulch around plants, such as straw or wood chips. Mulch retains moisture, regulates soil temperature, kills weeds, and enriches the soil with organic matter as it decomposes.
   - **Crop Rotation**: Practice crop rotation to prevent nutrient depletion and minimize disease and pest buildup. Rotate plant families or groups to different areas of the garden each year to maintain soil health and fertility.

The study of soil involves several different disciplines, including chemistry, hydrology, microbiology, physics, biology, and ecology.". This keeps the consistency in referring to soil as a general term. The term 'dirt' is often incorrectly used to refer to soil, leading to misunderstandings, as it connotes a lifeless and stagnant physical medium. Contrary to popular belief, soil is a dynamic, living, and ever-evolving natural ecosystem. The quality of the soil is the secret to a beautiful garden.

Responsible Water Usage (R): Techniques for Water Conservation While Maintaining a Vegetable Garden

Implementing water-saving techniques may drastically cut water usage while maintaining a healthy and productive vegetable garden, which is a crucial component of responsible gardening. Let's examine several methods for responsible water use (RWU) that encourage water conservation without interfering with your plants' ability to grow and develop.

1. **Drip Irrigation**: This technique employs a network of hoses or tubes that include emitters that gradually discharge water close to the plant's base. Drip irrigation minimizes waste and encourages the establishment of deep roots by ensuring that water reaches the roots where it is most required.

2. **Mulching**: Mulch serves as a shield, sheltering the soil from heat, wind, and sunshine and slowing down moisture loss. In addition, it aids in controlling soil temperature and inhibits weed development, lessening competition for water supplies. Mulch may be made from organic resources like compost, wood chips, or straw.

3. **Efficient Watering Schedules**: Water conservation depends on creating an effective watering schedule based on plant requirements and environmental considerations. Plants benefit from

infrequent but deep watering, as it encourages the formation of deep roots that can access water retained in the soil. Use a moisture meter to measure the moisture content of the soil or check it manually to keep track of it. Only water when absolutely essential, taking into account things like soil type, rainfall patterns, and plant water needs.

4. **Rainwater Harvesting**: A great strategy to preserve water and lessen dependency on other water sources is to use rainwater. To collect and store rainwater from roofs, use rain barrels or other rainwater collecting equipment. Use the water you've gathered to irrigate your vegetable garden when it's dry. Rainwater is perfect for hydrating plants since it is naturally devoid of chemicals.

5. **Plant Watering Techniques**: Adopting particular irrigation practices may help you save water even more while improving plant health. Avoid using overhead sprinklers, for instance, since they might cause water loss via evaporation and runoff. Instead, concentrate on giving the plant's base specific irrigation. Reduce water waste by using a watering can or hose with a low-flow nozzle to send water straight to the soil.

6. **Consideration of Environmental Factors**: Consider environmental factors that influence water requirements. Adjust irrigation practices during periods of increased precipitation or humidity. In general, plants require less frequent irrigation during periods of milder and more humid climate. During sweltering and arid conditions, you may need to increase the frequency or duration of irrigation to ensure adequate plant hydration.

To save water supplies and keep a vegetable garden healthy and productive, responsible water use is essential. You can maximize water use and support plant health by taking environmental elements into account and changing your watering tactics appropriately. Responsible water use, in addition to conserving this important resource, helps to promote sustainable gardening techniques. Use these strategies in your vegetable garden to balance water saving with plant hydration.

Selecting the Appropriate Tools and Equipment for Gardening

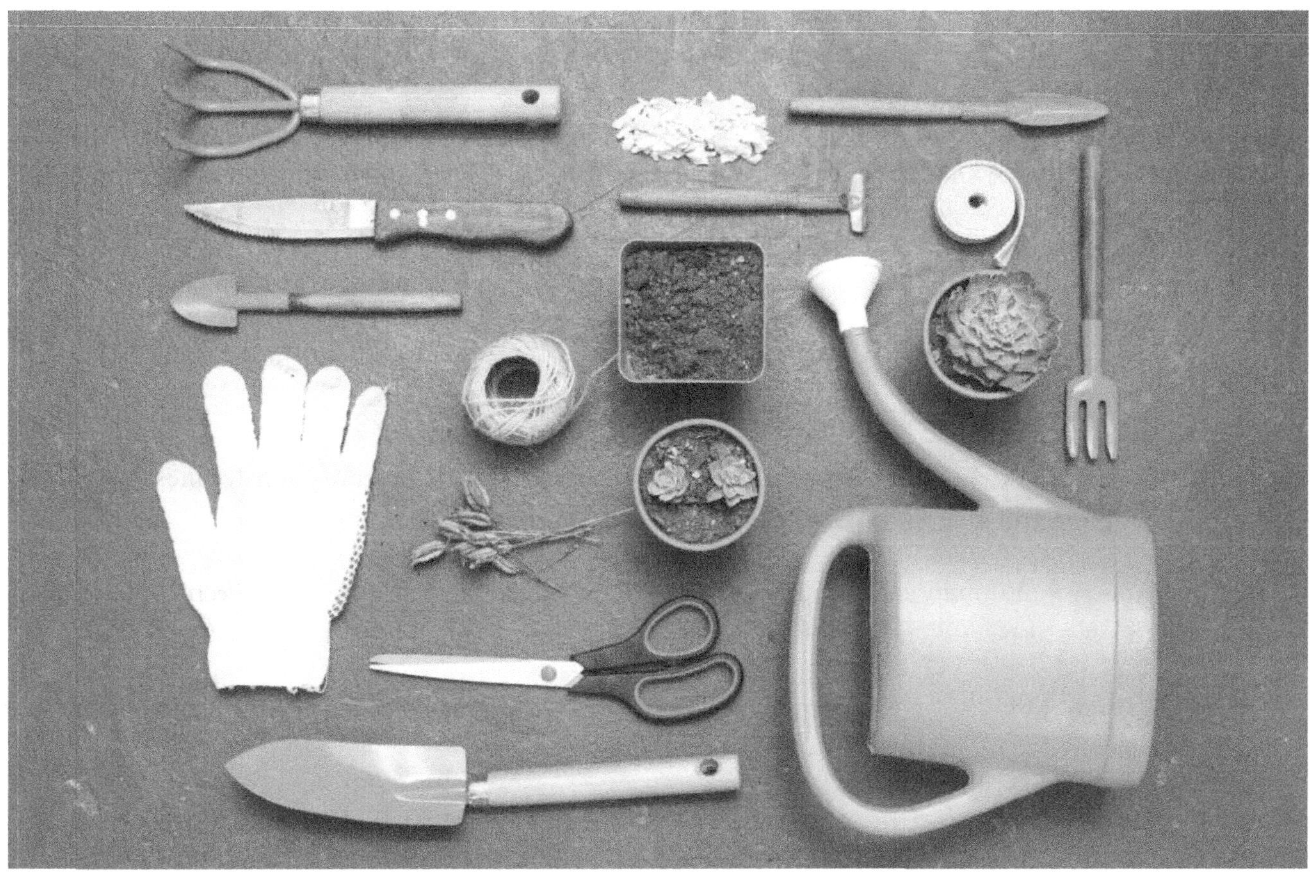

Vegetable growing success depends on having the appropriate tools and supplies. They simplify processes, boost productivity, and guarantee accuracy in a variety of gardening jobs. Let's examine the necessary tools and equipment for growing vegetables and discover how to choose them based on their quality, usefulness, and suitability for various gardening tasks.

1. **Hand Tools**: Hand tools are the backbone of any gardener's toolkit. Essential hand tools for vegetable gardening include:

    - **Trowel**: A small handheld shovel used for digging small holes, transplanting seedlings, and mixing soil amendments.

    - **Hand Fork**: A tool with multiple curved tines used for loosening soil, removing weeds, and breaking up clumps.

    - **Hand Pruners**: Also known as secateurs, these are used for pruning and trimming plants, removing dead or damaged foliage, and harvesting vegetables.

- **Hand Weeder**: A tool with a forked or hooked end for removing weeds from the root level, enabling precise weed control.
- **Hand Cultivator**: A handheld tool with multiple tines used for cultivating the soil, breaking up clods, and removing weeds.
- **Hand Rake**: A small rake with flexible tines, ideal for leveling soil, raking debris, and preparing seedbeds.

2. **Garden Implements**: Certain garden implements are invaluable for specific gardening tasks:

- **Shovel**: A sturdy shovel with a long handle and a pointed or square blade for digging large holes, moving soil, and transplanting plants.
- **Garden Fork**: A garden fork, which is akin to a pitchfork, features sturdy tines for stirring compost and integrating organic materials and for loosening compacted soil.
- **Hoe**: A multifunctional instrument with a sharp-edged blade used for weed removal, breaking up soil crusts, and cultivating the soil's surface.
- **Garden Knife**: A multi-purpose knife with a sharp blade for cutting twine, harvesting vegetables, and performing various garden tasks.

3. **Protective Gear**: Protective gear ensures your safety and comfort while working in the garden:

- **Gardening Gloves**: Durable gloves protect hands from thorns, prickly plants, and rough surfaces, while providing grip and dexterity.
- **Knee Pads**: Cushioned knee pads or a kneeling pad provide comfort and protect knees when kneeling or working close to the ground.
- **Hat and Sunscreen**: A wide-brimmed hat and sunscreen protect the face and neck from harmful UV rays during extended periods in the sun.
- **Protective Clothing**: Wearing long sleeves, long trousers, and closed-toe shoes protects against scratches, insect bites, and chemical exposure.

4. **Choosing Tools**: Consider the following factors when choosing tools for vegetable gardening:

- **Quality**: Invest in high-quality tools made from durable materials. They may cost more initially, but they tend to last longer and provide better performance.

- **Functionality**: Evaluate the functionality of each instrument. Ensure that they are ergonomically designed for simplicity of use and equipped with features that correspond to your horticulture requirements.

- **Suitability**: Based on your tasks, choose the right tools. Make sure the instruments are comfortable to hold for lengthy periods of time by taking into account their size and weight.

Before making a purchase, it's also a good idea to study product reviews, get suggestions from seasoned gardeners, and go to a nearby garden store to personally inspect and try out the equipment.

Having the right tools and equipment is crucial for successful vegetable farming. Prioritize tool quality, usability, and applicability for various gardening activities while making your selection. You can handle a variety of gardening tasks with the correct tools and equipment, and you may have a fruitful and satisfying vegetable garden as a result.

Understanding the Basics of Plant Growth and Development

In this book, we'll go through the fundamentals of planting and tending to a variety of vegetables. Let us delve into the intriguing phases of plant growth and the important components that impact plant development, shall we?

1. **Seed Germination**: A plant's life cycle starts with the germination of its seeds. A seed will absorb water when given the ideal circumstances (enough moisture, the right temperature, and oxygen), which will start biochemical reactions that result in the formation of a root, stem, and leaves. Beginning with germination, a plant begins its growth process.

2. **Vegetative Growth**: The plant concentrates on producing a strong root system, leaves, and stems during the vegetative development stage. The leaves conduct photosynthesis, converting sunlight into energy, while the roots absorb water and nutrients from the soil. Growing plants have larger leaf surfaces and a larger root system, which aid in food intake and energy generation.

3. **Reproductive Growth**: A plant enters reproductive development when it is prepared to produce blooms and, later, fruits or seeds. Light, temperature, and hormone signals are only a few of the variables that affect the change from vegetative to reproductive development. The growth of flowers enables pollination and fertilization, which result in the formation of seeds or fruits. The plant's life cycle is guaranteed to continue via reproductive development.

4. **Environmental Factors Affecting Plant Growth**: Several environmental factors influence plant growth and development. Understanding and managing such factors is crucial for optimal plant growth:

   - **Light**: Photosynthesis, the process through which plants convert sunlight into energy, relies on light. The appropriate quantity and quality of light are essential for a plant's development since different types of plants have different light needs.
   - **Temperature**: The physiological processes of plants are influenced by temperature. For optimum development, plants need precise temperature ranges. Temperature extremes may stress plants and have a detrimental effect on their growth.
   - **Nutrients**: Plants require essential nutrients for healthy growth. Macronutrients (nitrogen, phosphorus, potassium) and micronutrients (iron, zinc, magnesium) play crucial roles in plant metabolism and growth. Providing a balanced nutrient supply is essential for optimal plant development.
   - **Water**: The availability of sufficient water is essential for plant growth. Water aids in nutrient transport and maintains a plant's turgor, ensuring correct cell expansion and photosynthesis. To meet plants' water requirements without causing waterlogging or drought stress, proper irrigation techniques are required.
   - **Proper Care**: Pruning, fertilization, and vermin control are examples of maintenance practices. Pruning shapes plants, removes damaged or deceased portions, and increases ventilation. Fertilization guarantees that plants receive essential nutrients that are not naturally present in the soil. Pest management is the surveillance and control of vermin and diseases in order to prevent injury and promote healthy growth.

5. **Hormonal Regulation**: Additionally, hormones regulate plant growth and development. These chemical mediators regulate several physiological processes, such as cell division, elongation, and differentiation. Auxins, cytokinins, gibberellins, abscisic acid, and ethylene are the most important plant hormones. These hormones influence cell expansion, root development, flowering, and maturation to coordinate plant growth.

6. **Environmental Cues**: Plants respond to environmental signals including photoperiod (duration of daylight), temperature fluctuations, and seasonal changes. These stimuli initiate particular developmental processes, such as flowering and dormancy. Long-day plants, for instance, require a minimum amount of daylight to initiate flowering, whereas short-day plants bloom as daylight

hours decrease. Understanding these indicators enables cultivators to manipulate plant growth and flowering times, particularly in controlled environments or when cultivating crops out of season.

7. **Growth Habit and Form**: Different plants have different growth patterns, which have an impact on how they develop structurally. Certain plants are categorized as determinate, which means that their development pattern is fixed and they cease growing as soon as they reach a given size or begin to produce a certain number of flowers or fruits. Indeterminate plants continue to develop and provide fruit or blooms for a long time. Additionally, plants may grow in a variety of ways, such as shrubs, vines, or trees, which affects how they need to develop and how they should be managed.

8. **Genetic Factors**: The growth and development of plants are significantly influenced by genetics. Differentiations in features including growth rate, size, disease resistance, and fruit quality originate from genetic variants within plant species. To create new kinds with desirable qualities, plant breeding and genetic engineering methods are applied, enhancing productivity and adaptability to particular growing circumstances.

9. **Response to Environmental Stress**: Withstanding adaptation processes help plants deal with environmental stressors including drought, extreme heat, or nutrient deficiency. Changes in root architecture, the closing of stomata to lessen water loss, and the creation of protective chemicals are a few examples of these reactions. Gardeners may minimize the effects of unfavorable circumstances and maximize plant growth and survival by understanding these stress responses.

Having an understanding of how these variables interact and giving plants the ideal environment will help ensure their healthy growth and development.

Understanding the fundamentals of plant growth and development will enable you to better care for growing plants and help them flourish. You can encourage healthy development, optimize output, and take advantage of the beauty and advantages of a flourishing vegetable garden by creating the right circumstances and regulating these aspects.

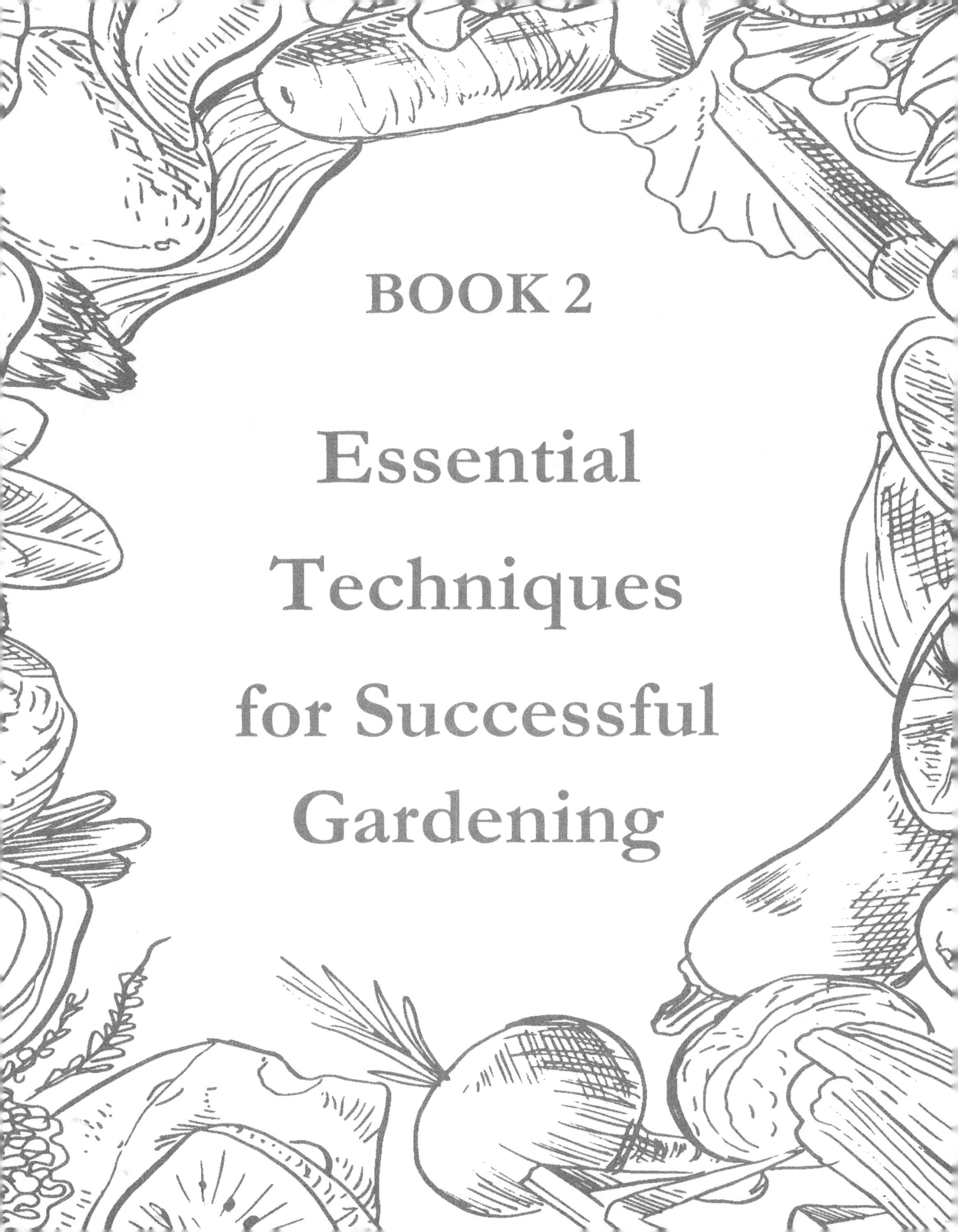

BOOK 2

Essential Techniques for Successful Gardening

Book 2: Essential Techniques for Successful Gardening

Introduction

A gratifying and enjoyable activity, gardening enables people to connect with nature, enhance their environment, and produce their own food. However, sowing seeds and hoping for the best is not enough to make a successful garden. It entails understanding and putting into practice a variety of fundamental procedures in order to guarantee healthy plant development, increase harvests, and foster a flourishing garden environment. This introduction will go over some of these crucial methods and how crucial they are to succeeding in gardening.

1. **Soil Preparation**: Preparing the soil is one of the key elements of gardening success. Essential nutrients, appropriate drainage, and an ideal environment for root growth are all provided by healthy soil. It is crucial to evaluate the soil type and make the necessary amendments. Compost or well-rotted manure are examples of organic matter that may be added to soil to help with fertility, moisture retention, and soil structure. An excellent foundation for plant development and general garden health is established by thorough soil preparation.

2. **Sunlight and Water Requirements**: For plants to be successfully grown, it is essential to understand their needs for water and sunshine. The majority of plants need enough sunshine to flourish, however

precise light needs might vary. While some plants like full light, others do well in little shade. Similar to this, different plant species have different water needs. Root rot or plant dehydration may result from either overwatering or underwatering. By being aware of the particular requirements of your plants, you can guarantee that they get the proper quantity of water and light for optimum development.

3. **Plant Selection and Placement**: Selecting the proper vegetation for your garden is crucial to your horticulture success. Climate, soil conditions, and available space should be considered when selecting vegetation. Some plants are better adapted to particular climates or varieties of soil, while others require more space to grow. In addition, knowing the growth patterns and mature proportions of plants helps determine their placement in the garden. Appropriate plant selection and placement guarantee that each plant has sufficient space to develop and flourish.

4. **Mulching**: Mulching involves applying a layer of organic or inorganic material around plants to conserve water, inhibit weed growth, and regulate soil temperature. Straw, wood shavings, and compost are examples of organic mulches that decompose over time to enrich the soil with nutrients. Mulching creates a favorable microclimate for plant roots, reducing evaporation of water and vegetation competition. It is an effective method for maintaining soil health and reducing garden maintenance duties.

5. **Pruning and Training**: Techniques of pruning and training are essential for maintaining the health and form of plants. Pruning is the process of removing deceased, diseased, or overgrown branches to promote new growth and enhance air circulation. The use of training techniques, such as staking or trellising, assists in sustaining plants with feeble stems or climbers. Pruning and training not only foster plant health, but also increase the garden's aesthetic appeal.

6. **Pest and Disease Management**: One of the most common challenges in gardening is overcoming the problems presented by diseases and pests. It is very essential to safeguard plants from harm by putting into practice efficient ways for managing pests and diseases. This includes early identification of pests and diseases, utilizing natural or organic pest control methods, and maintaining a high level of cleanliness in the garden. The health of the soil can be significantly improved by carefully selecting and rotating crops.

7. **Regular Maintenance and Care**: Maintaining and caring for a garden throughout time is essential to its success. It is vital for optimum development to do routine duties like as watering, weeding, fertilizing, and checking the overall health of the plant. It is essential to establish a regimen for gardening and to remain dedicated to doing upkeep on a consistent basis. In addition, making sure you are up to date on the best gardening practices for each season and modifying your methods appropriately may assist assure success throughout the whole year.

Applying crucial methods that support plant health, increase yields, and design a beautiful landscape is key for successful gardening. Gardeners may position themselves for gardening success by comprehending and putting into practice soil preparation, appropriate plant selection, watering and sunshine needs, mulching, pruning and training, pest and disease control, and routine maintenance. These methods help people appreciate the beauty and benefits of their gardening efforts and provide the groundwork for a healthy garden.

Proper Techniques for and Transplanting Seedlings

Proper techniques for sowing seeds and transplanting seedlings are crucial for successful gardening. Your chances of successfully growing plants from seeds and transplanting young seedlings into garden beds or containers will significantly improve. Let's explore these techniques in detail.

Sowing Seeds:

1. **Seed Selection**: Choose high-quality seeds from a reputable supplier. Consider factors such as plant variety, disease resistance, and suitability to your climate and growing conditions.
2. **Timing**: Determine the appropriate time to sow seeds based on the specific requirements of each plant. Some seeds can be directly sown outdoors, while others benefit from indoor seed starting and later transplantation.
3. **Soil Preparation**: Use a seed-starting mix or a well-draining, sterile potting. Avoid using regular garden soil as it may contain pathogens and hinder seed germination. Mix organic matter, such as compost, into the soil to improve its fertility.
4. **Seed Depth and Spacing**: Follow the seed packet instructions for the recommended planting depth and spacing between seeds. Generally, smaller seeds require shallow planting, while larger seeds can be planted deeper.

5. **Germination Conditions**: Place the seeded containers in a warm and well-lit location. Most seeds require consistent moisture to germinate, so water them gently and ensure the soil remains moist but not waterlogged. Using a plastic cover or a humidity dome can help create a suitable microclimate.
6. **Transplanting Seedlings**: Once the seedlings have grown sufficiently and the weather conditions are appropriate for outdoor planting, it's time to transplant them into your garden beds or containers.
7. **Harden off Seedlings**: Before transplanting, gradually expose the seedlings to outdoor conditions over a period of 7-10 days. Start with a few hours of exposure to direct sunlight and increase the duration each day. This process helps the seedlings acclimate to temperature fluctuations, wind, and sunlight.
8. **Soil Preparation**: Prepare the planting area by removing weeds and loosening the soil. Incorporate organic matter to improve soil structure and fertility.
9. **Digging the Hole**: Dig a hole slightly larger than the root ball of the seedling. Gently loosen the soil around the hole to aid in root penetration.
10. **Transplanting**: Carefully remove the seedling from its container by holding the leaves or gently tapping the bottom. Avoid pulling the plant by the stem, as it can damage delicate roots. Place the seedling in the hole, ensuring it sits at the same depth as it was in its container. Backfill the hole with soil, lightly firming it around the roots.
11. **Watering and Mulching**: After transplanting, water the seedlings thoroughly to settle the soil and promote root establishment. Apply a layer of organic mulch, such as straw or wood chips, to help retain moisture and suppress weed growth.

Wise Crop Selection and Rotation

Crop selection and rotation, which play a crucial role in maximizing yield and maintaining soil health, require consideration of the following factors.

1. **Diversity**: Choose a mix of crops that have different growth habits, nutrient requirements, and maturity dates. This helps reduce the risk of pests and diseases and ensures a continuous supply of fresh produce throughout the season.

2. **Companion Planting**: Select crops that are compatible and benefit each other when grown together. Some plants repel pests, while others enhance nutrient uptake or provide shade.

3. **Crop Rotation**: Rotate crops within your garden beds or containers each year. Avoid planting the same family of plants in the same area consecutively, as it can lead to nutrient imbalances and increase the likelihood of pests and diseases. Instead, follow a rotation schedule that moves plants through different sections or containers over several years.

By implementing these proper techniques, you can enhance your gardening success, from sowing seeds and raising seedlings to choosing the right crops and practicing rotation. Remember to adapt these techniques to suit your specific growing conditions and follow best practices for the particular plants you are working with.

Wise Crop Selection and Rotation (W): Maximizing Yield through Strategic Crop Choices

To enhance productivity, maintain soil health and prevent the spread of pests and To enhance productivity, maintain soil health, and prevent the spread of pests and diseases, it is crucial to implement strategies such as careful crop selection and rotation.

By understanding the needs of each plant considering variations and adapting to different climates we can delve into the importance of crop rotation and selection.

1. Soil Health Preservation; The choice of crops and implementing crop rotation plays a role in preserving soil health. Every crop has its requirements and repeatedly planting the same crop in the same area can deplete specific nutrients from the soil over time. This depletion can lead to imbalances, reduced fertility and lower yields.

Farmers have found that by rotating their crops they can break this cycle of depletion. Through alternating between crops farmers can minimize nutrient loss while allowing the soil to replenish gradually. It's worth noting that various plants have different demands. For instance leguminous plants like peas and beans have nitrogen fixing abilities that replenish nitrogen levels in the soil by converting nitrogen into a form for other plants.

Crop rotation also plays a role, in preventing soil erosion. Rooted plants help stabilize the soil structure while minimizing erosion caused by wind or water flow. Additionally, diversifying crops enhances activity within the soil, improving its overall fertility and health..

2. Managing Pests and Diseases; Crop rotation and careful crop selection are methods, for controlling pests and diseases. When the same crop is cultivated in the area repeatedly it creates an environment that encourages the growth of pests and illnesses. Over time these pests and diseases can build up populations as they specifically target plant hosts.

To disrupt the life cycles of pests and diseases farmers can rotate their crops making it harder for them to establish and multiply. By alternating crops with susceptibilities to pests and diseases farmers can reduce the chances of infestations. Additionally some plants act as deterrents or trap plants that divert pests away from the crops minimizing damage.

3. Choosing the Right Vegetables for Your Garden; To ensure a harvest, with yield several factors should be considered when selecting vegetables for your garden;

a) **Climate**; Different crops thrive in different types of climates. Some prefer certain temperatures while others do well in other ranges. It's important to understand your climate to choose vegetables that will grow effectively and produce yields.

b) **Seasonality**; Different vegetables have their growing seasons, so it's important to choose crops that align with the local season for better chances of success For example summer is ideal for warm season crops like tomatoes and peppers while spring or fall is better suited for cool season crops like lettuce and spinach.

c) **Specific Plant Requirements**; Vegetables have varying needs when it comes to sunlight, soil type, moisture and spacing. Considering these factors is essential to ensure growth and yield. While some veggies thrive in sun others can tolerate shade. Additionally, different crops may require specific soil fertility levels and pH.

d) **Succession Planting**; To maximize yield throughout the growing season you can employ succession planting techniques. This involves planting crops in stages with different maturation dates. By doing this, instead of having one harvest, you'll have a continuous supply of fresh produce

e) **Crop Compatibility**; When certain plants are grown together they can interact in ways. For instance, planting herbs like basil or marigolds near tomatoes can help repel pests. However it's important to be aware that some crops may compete for resources or attract pests when planted together—understanding companion planting is crucial.

To improve productivity and maintain soil health it is crucial to make choices when selecting and rotating crops. Farmers and gardeners should carefully consider factors like the environment, suitability, and specific plant needs in order to choose the most suitable vegetables for their requirements. Crop rotation plays a role in preventing the buildup of pests and diseases, preserving nutrient levels in the soil, and promoting overall soil health These practices contribute to fruitful systems.

Responsible Water Usage (R): Efficient Irrigation Methods for Sustainable Gardening

Responsible water usage is a crucial aspect of sustainable gardening, and efficient irrigation methods play a significant role in minimizing water waste while ensuring proper plant hydration. By adopting innovative irrigation techniques and understanding the water needs of different crops, gardeners can create customized irrigation schedules for optimal plant growth. Let's delve into some of these methods and concepts.

1. **Drip Irrigation**: Drip irrigation is a method that delivers water directly to the roots of plants, thus reducing water loss due to evaporation and runoff. It involves the use of tubing with small holes or emitters placed near the plants, allowing water to drip slowly onto the soil. Drip irrigation ensures that water reaches the plants' root zones precisely, reducing water waste and promoting healthier root development.

2. **Soaker Hoses**: Soaker hoses, also known as permeable hoses, are another good choice for water-efficient irrigation. These hoses are porous and release water directly into the soil, providing a slow, even, and targeted watering. By laying soaker hoses along the base of plants or in garden beds, water is delivered directly to the root zones, preventing water loss due to evaporation and runoff.

3. **Water-Saving Technologies**: Advancements in technology have led to the development of various water-saving tools and systems that can be employed in gardening. Installing soil moisture sensors in the garden allows you to determine the amount of water present in the soil. These sensors can help determine when and how much water should be applied, preventing overwatering and conserving water.

4. **Understanding Crop Water Needs**: Different crops have varying water requirements based on factors such as their stage of growth, root depth, and environmental conditions. It is important to understand these water needs to avoid both over and under watering. Conducting research or consulting reliable sources can provide valuable information about the specific water requirements of various plants. By tailoring irrigation practices to meet the needs of specific crops, gardeners can avoid wasting water.

5. **Customized Irrigation Schedules**: Creating customized irrigation schedules is essential for sustainable gardening. Gardeners can develop individualized irrigation plans for maximum plant growth by using cutting-edge irrigation methods and understanding the water requirements of various crops. Adjusting irrigation frequency, duration, and timing based on these factors can help optimize plant growth and minimize water usage.

Organic Pest and Disease Control (O): Eco-Friendly Practices for Maintaining Plant Health

In this section, we'll provide a concise overview of eco-friendly pesticides, emphasizing their significance in maintaining plant health naturally and sustainably. We'll delve into the realm of organic pest and disease control, exploring methods that prioritize the well-being of your garden while minimizing environmental impact. Through the following sections, we'll delve deeper into specific strategies and solutions to address various plant-related challenges.

Identifying Common Plant Issues:

To effectively address plant health, it's crucial to be aware of the potential problems that can arise. Gardeners often encounter a range of challenges that can impede the growth and vitality of plants. Some of the most prevalent issues include:

- **Pests**: Insects, mites, and other pests can inflict harm on leaves, stems, and fruits, leading to diminished plant health and productivity.
- **Diseases**: Fungal, bacterial, and viral infections can weaken plants, causing symptoms like discoloration, wilting, and even plant death.

- **Nutrient Deficiencies**: Insufficient nutrients can result in stunted growth, yellowing leaves, and poor fruit formation.
- **Environmental Stress**: Extreme temperatures, drought, excessive moisture, and poor soil conditions can stress plants and make them vulnerable to various problems.
- **Weeds**: Unwanted plants compete for resources and can overtake desired plants.

By recognizing these potential challenges, you'll be better equipped to proactively prevent and address them, ensuring the health and vitality of your plants.

Eco-Friendly Pest and Disease Solutions

When it comes to maintaining the health of your plants while also being mindful of the environment, eco-friendly pesticides offer effective alternatives to conventional chemical treatments. These natural solutions harness the power of nature itself to combat pests and diseases. Here are some eco-friendly options and how they can help address common plant issues:

- **Neem Oil**: Derived from the neem tree, neem oil acts as both an insect repellent and an antifeedant. It disrupts the life cycle of insects by affecting their feeding and reproduction.
- **Diatomaceous Earth**: Made from fossilized diatoms, diatomaceous earth is a powder that damages the exoskeletons of insects, causing dehydration and death.
- **Insecticidal Soap**: This soap targets soft-bodied insects like aphids, mealybugs, and mites. It suffocates pests by coating them in a soapy film, disrupting their ability to breathe.
- **Pyrethrin**: Extracted from chrysanthemum flowers, pyrethrin is a natural insecticide that paralyzes and kills a variety of pests on contact.
- **Bacillus Thuringiensis (Bt)**: This bacterium produces proteins toxic to specific insect larvae, making it a valuable tool against caterpillars and mosquitoes.
- **Beneficial Nematodes**: These microscopic organisms prey on soil-dwelling insects and larvae, effectively reducing pest populations.
- **Copper-Based Fungicides**: Used to combat fungal diseases, copper-based solutions create an inhospitable environment for pathogens.
- **Garlic Spray**: Garlic contains natural sulfur compounds that deter pests and also has antifungal properties.
- **Companion Planting**: Certain plants, when grown together, can deter pests or attract beneficial insects that control pests.

These eco-friendly solutions offer a targeted approach to pest and disease management, minimizing harm to beneficial insects, soil health, and overall ecosystem balance. Incorporating these options into your gardening practices supports the long-term health and vitality of your plants without compromising the environment.

Integrated Pest Management (IPM)

Integrated Pest Management (IPM) is a comprehensive and sustainable approach to pest and disease control that emphasizes prevention, monitoring, and the use of multiple strategies to manage garden challenges. Unlike traditional methods that rely heavily on chemical treatments, IPM takes a holistic approach that considers the entire ecosystem, including the interactions between plants, pests, beneficial insects, and the environment.

The key components of IPM include:

- **Prevention**: The first line of defense is preventing pests and diseases from establishing themselves in the garden. This involves choosing pest-resistant plant varieties, practicing good hygiene, and creating optimal growing conditions.
- **Identification and Monitoring**: Regularly inspecting your plants for signs of pests, diseases, or nutrient imbalances is crucial. Early detection helps prevent the escalation of problems.
- **Cultural Practices**: IPM encourages the use of cultural practices that promote plant health and minimize vulnerabilities. This includes proper watering, pruning, and providing adequate spacing to reduce conditions conducive to disease.
- **Biological Control**: Beneficial insects and predators can be introduced to control pest populations naturally. For instance, ladybugs prey on aphids, while parasitic wasps target caterpillars.
- **Mechanical Control**: Physical barriers, like row covers, can prevent insects from accessing plants. Hand-picking larger pests, such as caterpillars, is also part of this strategy.
- **Chemical Control**: If necessary, IPM includes the targeted use of eco-friendly pesticides. However, chemical control is a last resort and is applied judiciously to minimize harm to non-target organisms.
- **Education and Record Keeping**: Keeping track of garden activities, pest and disease occurrences, and the success of various control methods helps refine your IPM strategy over time.

By integrating these practices, gardeners can strike a balance between managing pests and maintaining a healthy ecosystem. IPM not only reduces the reliance on chemicals but also promotes long-term sustainability and resilience in your garden. This approach empowers you to make informed decisions, adapt strategies as needed, and create a thriving garden that harmoniously coexists with nature.

The Importance of Soil Health in Preventing Plant Problems:

A strong and vibrant garden starts from the ground up – with the health of your soil. Soil health plays a pivotal role in preventing a range of plant problems, from pests to diseases. Understanding the intricate relationship between soil and plants is essential for successful gardening and sustainable pest management.

Healthy soil provides several benefits that contribute to plant resilience:

- **Nutrient Availability**: Soil rich in organic matter hosts a diverse community of microorganisms that break down organic materials into nutrients that plants can absorb. This availability of essential nutrients directly contributes to strong plant growth and immune systems.
- **Plant Immunity**: Well-balanced soil promotes strong plant root systems, which, in turn, enhances the plants' ability to defend against pests and diseases. Nutrient-rich soil helps plants produce compounds that deter pests and encourage beneficial microorganisms that outcompete harmful ones.

- **Water Management**: Healthy soil structure retains moisture while allowing excess water to drain, reducing the risk of waterlogged roots and root diseases. Adequate drainage also discourages the proliferation of fungus and molds.
- **Biodiversity**: A thriving soil ecosystem supports a diverse community of microorganisms, including those that naturally control pests. These beneficial organisms can help keep pest populations in check and maintain ecological balance.
- **pH Balance**: Soil pH influences nutrient availability and plant health. Proper pH levels enable plants to access nutrients effectively, while extreme pH levels can lead to nutrient imbalances and weaken plants.
- **Resilience to Stress**: Healthy soil helps plants withstand stressors like extreme temperatures, drought, and other environmental challenges. Strong, resilient plants are less susceptible to infestations and diseases.

To enhance soil health and prevent plant problems, adopt practices that foster soil vitality. Adding organic matter like compost, cover cropping, practicing no-till gardening, and avoiding over-fertilization with synthetic chemicals are all ways to improve soil structure and microbial diversity.

By prioritizing soil health, you establish a foundation for a robust garden ecosystem where plants thrive naturally, requiring fewer interventions to combat pests and diseases. A holistic approach that encompasses both the aboveground and belowground realms of your garden will ultimately lead to the successful prevention of many common plant problems.

Beneficial Insects and Predators

Nature provides an arsenal of allies to aid in the battle against garden pests – beneficial insects and predators. These tiny heroes play a crucial role in maintaining a balanced and healthy ecosystem within your garden. By harnessing the power of these natural allies, you can effectively reduce the populations of harmful pests without resorting to harmful chemicals. Here are some key players in this insect army:

- **Ladybugs (Lady Beetles)**: These charming insects are voracious consumers of aphids, mealybugs, and mites. A single ladybug can devour hundreds of pests in a day, making them invaluable for keeping garden pests in check.
- **Parasitoid Wasps**: These tiny wasps lay their eggs in or on the bodies of harmful insects. When the wasp larvae hatch, they consume the host from the inside, effectively eliminating the pest. Examples include braconid wasps and trichogramma wasps.
- **Lacewings**: Lacewing larvae are aggressive predators of aphids, caterpillars, and other soft-bodied insects. They are easily recognized by their large, delicate wings and ferocious appetite for pests.
- **Praying Mantises**: These stealthy predators are known for their distinctive appearance and voracious appetite for a wide variety of insects, including beetles, flies, and even other mantises.
- **Predatory Nematodes**: These microscopic worms attack and feed on soil-dwelling pests, such as grubs and root-feeding larvae. They can be applied to the soil as a biological control measure.
- **Ground Beetles**: Nocturnal ground beetles are skilled hunters that prey on a range of pests, including slugs, snails, and insect eggs. Their presence is often a sign of a healthy garden ecosystem.

- **Hoverflies**: These harmless flies resemble bees but are effective pollinators and voracious consumers of aphids and other soft-bodied insects.

To attract and support beneficial insects, create a garden environment that offers food, shelter, and water. Plant diverse flowering plants that provide nectar and pollen for adult beneficials. Incorporating native plants and maintaining some undisturbed areas can also encourage these insects to take up residence in your garden.

It's important to note that the use of chemical pesticides can harm beneficial insects along with the pests. Embracing a more holistic approach by encouraging these natural predators is a win-win strategy that helps maintain a healthy garden ecosystem while reducing the need for chemical interventions.

Homemade Remedies for Pest and Disease Control

Harnessing the power of common household ingredients, homemade remedies offer effective solutions for managing pests and diseases without resorting to harsh chemicals. These DIY concoctions are easy to prepare, environmentally friendly, and safe for both your plants and beneficial insects. Here are some tried-and-true homemade remedies to consider:

- **Soap Spray**: A simple mixture of mild liquid soap and water can suffocate soft-bodied insects like aphids, mites, and whiteflies. Spray the solution directly onto the pests to control their population.
- **Oil Spray**: Vegetable oils like canola or olive oil, combined with soap and water, create an effective insect-smothering spray. This remedy is particularly useful for treating scales, mites, and mealybugs.
- **Baking Soda Spray**: Mixing baking soda, water, and a bit of soap forms a solution that helps control fungal diseases like powdery mildew and black spot on leaves.
- **Epsom Salt Solution**: Epsom salt, when dissolved in water, can provide magnesium to plants and deter pests like slugs. It's a double benefit for both plant nutrition and pest control.
- **Chili Pepper Spray**: Infuse heat into your garden defenses with a spicy spray made from hot chili peppers and water. This remedy is effective against mammals, insects, and even certain fungal infections.
- **Citrus Peel Spray**: Boiling citrus peels in water and then straining the solution creates a natural deterrent for ants, aphids, and other small insects.
- **Vinegar Solution**: A diluted solution of vinegar and water can help control fungal diseases on leaves and discourage pests like ants and fruit flies.
- **Milk Spray**: Diluted milk has been found to suppress powdery mildew and other fungal infections while providing some nutrients to plants.
- **Beer Traps**: For slugs and snails, set up shallow containers filled with beer. These pests are attracted to the scent, crawl in, and drown.
- **Onion and Garlic Spray**: Blend chopped onions and garlic with water to create a potent repellent spray against a wide range of pests.

Remember, the effectiveness of homemade remedies may vary depending on the specific pests and diseases in your garden. It's essential to test a small area of your plants before applying any remedy widely to ensure your plants tolerate the solution. Regular application and consistency are key to achieving the desired results. Additionally, rotating different remedies can help prevent pests from developing resistance. Always monitor your plants for signs of improvement or any adverse effects.

Monitoring and Early Detection

Vigilance is a gardener's best friend when it comes to managing pests and diseases. Regular monitoring and early detection play a crucial role in preventing infestations from spiraling out of control. Here's how you can effectively keep tabs on your garden's health:

- **Frequent Inspections**: Regularly inspect your plants for any signs of trouble. Look for chewed leaves, discolored foliage, wilting, or any unusual growth patterns. Early intervention can make a significant difference.
- **Use Sticky Traps**: Place sticky traps near plants susceptible to flying insects. These traps capture adult pests and help you identify potential problems before they escalate.
- **Check the Undersides**: Many pests prefer hiding on the undersides of leaves. Gently lift the leaves and examine them closely for pests, eggs, or larvae.
- **Use Hand Lens**: A hand lens or magnifying glass can help you spot tiny pests that might be difficult to see with the naked eye.
- **Learn Pest Life Cycles**: Understanding the life cycles of common pests in your region can help you anticipate their arrival and take preventive measures.
- **Record Keeping**: Maintain a garden journal noting when you planted, fertilized, and observed any issues. This record can help you identify patterns and trends over time.
- **Neighborhood Watch**: Keep an eye on neighboring gardens. Pests can easily move from one garden to another, so being aware of local infestations can help you take preemptive action.
- **Beneficial Insects**: Regularly inspect for beneficial insects like ladybugs, lacewings, and parasitic wasps. They can help keep pest populations in check.
- **Digital Resources**: Use online resources, apps, or community forums to identify pests and diseases you might not be familiar with.
- **Quarantine New Plants**: Before introducing new plants to your garden, quarantine them for a period to ensure they are free from pests or diseases.

By closely observing your garden and catching problems early, you can address issues promptly with less impact on your plants and ecosystem. Remember, the goal is to maintain a balanced environment where beneficial organisms can thrive and keep pests in check naturally. Your attentiveness and care will be rewarded with a healthier, more vibrant garden.

Fertilization Practices and Using Organic Alternatives

Soil fertility plays a role, in the well being and productivity of plants. It refers to the ability of the soil to provide nutrients and support plant growth. To maintain and enhance soil fertility, it is important to adopt fertilization techniques that prioritize sustainable alternatives. Natural amendments, composting and organic fertilizers are methods for supplying plants with the nutrients while promoting environmentally friendly and sustainable gardening practices.

Organic Fertilizers

Organic fertilizers, derived from natural sources, contain a variety of minerals that are essential for plant growth.. These fertilizers are often produced using ingredients like compost, manure, bone meal, fish emulsion, seaweed and other elements obtained from plants and animals. Here are some advantages associated with using organic fertilizers;

1. **Gradual nutrient release**; Organic fertilizers release nutrients slowly over time, ensuring a steady supply for plants. This minimizes the risk of fertilizer burn and prevents nutrient imbalances.

2. **Improved soil structure**; Organic fertilizers enhance the properties of the soil by increasing its capacity to retain nutrients and water. They also promote activity that enhances soil aeration, structure and nutrient cycling.

Nutrient Diversity

Nutrient diversity plays a role in agriculture as it ensures that plants receive a balanced amount of minerals Organic fertilizers, which consist of both micronutrients like iron, zinc and manganese and macronutrients like nitrogen, phosphorus and potassium provide this range of nutrients.

Environmental Sustainability

One of the advantages of organic fertilizers is their contribution to environmental sustainability. These fertilizers are derived from renewable resources and undergo minimal processing. By reducing reliance on fertilizers that can harm the environment through soil erosion and water contamination organic fertilizers promote an eco-friendly approach.

Composting

Composting is another technique used in agriculture. It involves decomposing waste materials such as kitchen scraps, yard trimmings and plant leftovers into nutrient rich compost. This compost improves soil fertility, structure, moisture retention capacity while also enhancing activity for better plant health and nutrient cycling.

Natural Amendments

In addition to composting natural amendments are commonly used to address soil qualities or deficiencies. For example rock phosphate serves as a source of phosphorus while gypsum and limestone help adjust the pH levels of the soil. These natural mineral-based supplements prove effective in resolving soil imbalances or deficiencies.

Proper Methods and Timing

To ensure results when applying fertilizers and amendments to your plants it is crucial to follow proper methods and timing guidelines.

Here are some suggestions to consider;

1. Start by conducting a soil test to determine the pH levels and nutrient content. This will help you identify any imbalances or deficiencies allowing you to select the fertilizers and additives.

2. Follow the recommended application rates provided by either the manufacturer or your own soil test results. Using excessive amounts of fertilizer can lead to nutrient runoff and harm the environment

3. Timing is crucial when it comes to applying fertilizers and amendments. Consider the requirements of your plants and apply them accordingly. Some fertilizers should be sprayed before planting while others can be used throughout the growing season.

4. Utilize mulches, around your plants as they serve purposes such as retaining moisture preventing weed growth and gradually releasing nutrients into the soil.

5. Ensure incorporation of fertilizers and amendments into the soil by thoroughly mixing them in for even distribution and maximum contact with plant roots.

Maintaining soil fertility is vital for plant growth and productivity. Implementing methods like using organic fertilizers, composting, and amendments not only provide plants with essential nutrients but also promote environmentally friendly gardening practices By utilizing application techniques and recognizing the benefits of alternatives gardeners can effectively care for their plants while contributing positively to the environment.

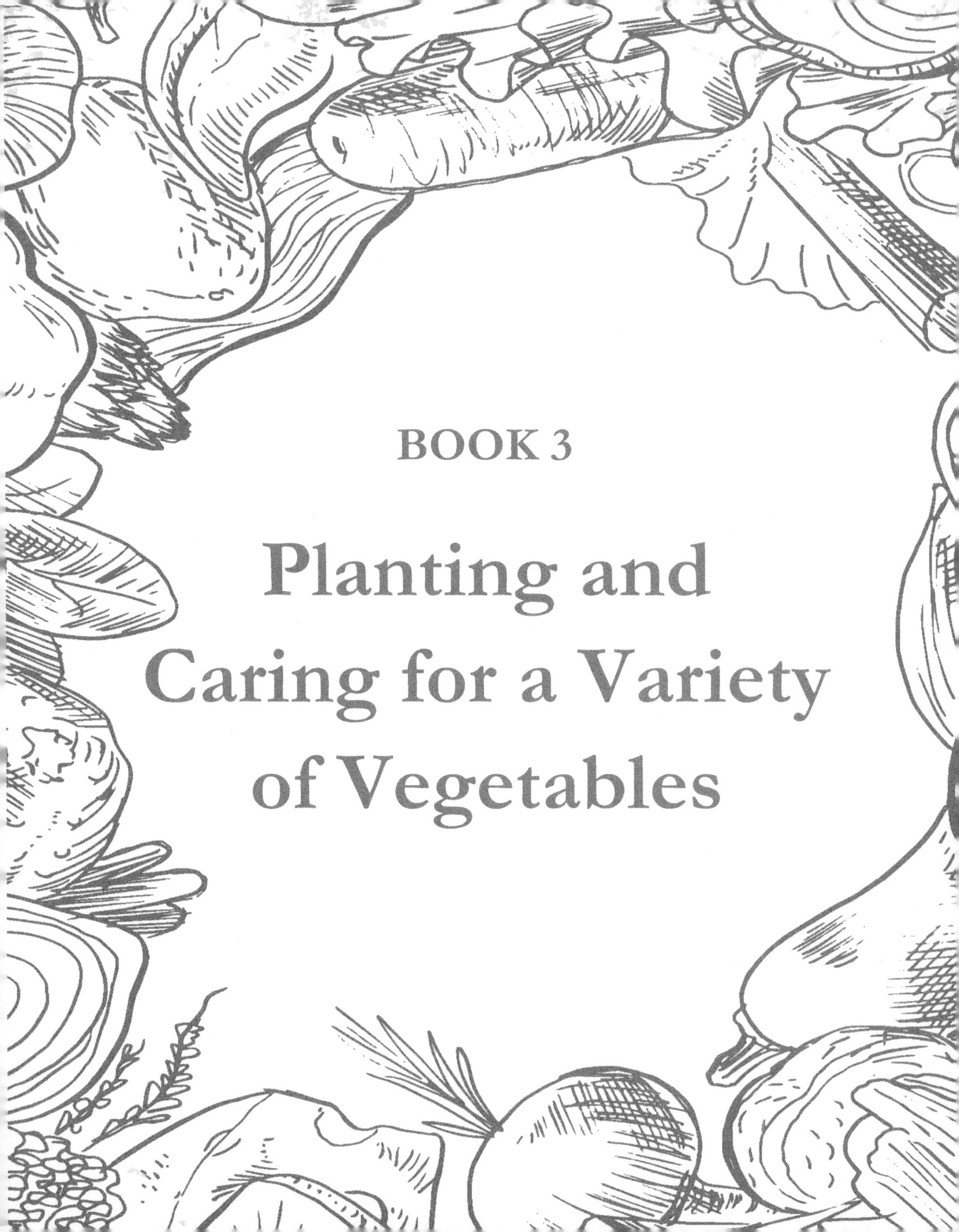

BOOK 3

Planting and Caring for a Variety of Vegetables

Book 3: Planting and Caring for a Variety of Vegetables

Introduction

Vegetable gardening can be a pastime that requires dedication, time and hard work. It's a way to ensure a supply of fresh and organic food regardless of whether you have a vast garden or just enough space for container gardening. Let's explore the steps involved in planting and caring for types of vegetables.

Plan and Prepare

To begin with it's important to plan and prepare your garden before diving into the planting process. Take into consideration the area, sunlight exposure, soil quality and the specific needs of the vegetables you wish to cultivate. Ensuring that your chosen spot receives at least six to eight hours of sunlight daily is crucial.

Soil Preparation

For vegetables to thrive they require soil that drains well. Clear any weeds, rocks or other debris from the soil. Enhancing soil fertility and structure can be achieved by incorporating organic matter such as compost or rotted manure. Additionally it may be helpful to assess the pH level and nutrient content of the soil and make adjustments based on the results.

Choose Suitable Crops

Lastly select crops that are well suited for your region while also satisfying your preferences and offering an opportunity for gardening skills growth. Starting off with tried and true options like tomatoes, cucumbers, lettuce, carrots, peppers and herbs, like basil and parsley is a great way to begin your vegetable gardening journey.

Understand the Needs of Each Plant

To ensure the success of your vegetable garden it's crucial to understand the needs of each plant. Different types of vegetables have varying planting times based on your location. Some may require starting seeds indoors, then transplanting them later. To determine the spacing and depth for planting refer to the information provided on seed packaging or plant labels.

Proper Watering

When it comes to watering it's essential to provide hydration for vegetables to thrive. On average they need 1-1.5 inches of water per week. This requirement may vary depending on climate conditions and growth stages. To promote root development. Prevent disease transmission to leaves ensure regular and thorough watering targeted at the base of the plants.

Consistent Fertilization

Since vegetables are feeders, consistent fertilization is key for their well being. You can incorporate slow-release balanced fertilizer into the soil before planting or enrich it with organic matter. Additionally liquid fertilizers and foliar sprays can be used throughout the growing season to supplement soil nutrients.

Weed Control

Lastly controlling weeds is crucial as they compete with your veggies, for water, sunlight and nutrients. Make sure to water your plants especially when it's dry outside. Adding a layer of mulch will help retain moisture in the soil and prevent water loss.

Pest and Disease Management

Keep an eye out for aphids, caterpillars and snails as they can harm your plants. To manage pests and diseases effectively (step eight) be vigilant, in monitoring your vegetable garden. You can control pest populations through methods like practices organic sprays or introducing beneficial insects.

Harvest at Peak Maturity

For the taste, harvest your vegetables at their peak maturity. Look for signs such, as color, size or texture to know when they are ready to be picked. Regular harvesting not only ensures production but also stimulates new growth.

Learn and Adapt

Remember that gardening is a learning process. Different vegetables have requirements, so it's important to experiment and observe closely. Adjust your methods accordingly based on what you learn along the way. With time and effort you'll become an expert vegetable grower. Enjoy the fruits (or vegetables) of your labor!

Comprehensive Profiles of Popular Vegetables, Including Their Specific Needs and Growth Habits

Below you will find descriptions of vegetables and their optimal growing conditions.

- **Tomatoes**
  Firstly, let's talk about tomatoes. These warm season crops thrive when they receive an amount of sunlight around 6 8 hours, per day. To ensure their growth and development it is recommended to plant tomatoes in soil with a pH level ranging from 6.0 to 6.8. It is important that the soil is well drained and enriched with matter. When starting tomato plants from transplants it is advisable to space them 2 3 feet. Regular and deep watering twice a week is essential for their proper hydration. Many gardeners use cages or stakes as supports to encourage growth.

- **Cucumbers**
  Next up are cucumbers which share requirements as tomatoes in terms of sunlight exposure. These vine growing plants flourish when planted in full sun throughout the growing months For growth cucumbers prefer acidic to neutral soil with a pH level between 6.0 and 7.0; loose and well-drained soil is ideal for them too! You have two options for planting cucumbers; you sow the seeds directly into your garden. Start them indoors before transferring them outside later on. Cucumbers need watering during dry periods

so make sure they receive enough moisture. Applying a layer of mulch can help retain moisture in the soil. If you want your cucumbers to climb trellises or prefer letting them sprawl on the ground, it's entirely up to you!

- **Peppers (Bell Peppers and Chili Peppers)**
  Lastly let's discuss peppers such, as bell peppers and chili peppers which are commonly grown during the summer months; these varieties require direct sunlight exposure. Peppers prefer soil with a pH range of 6.0 to 6.8 and its important to ensure good drainage. Starting pepper seeds indoors is advantageous as it allows for transplantation once the soil has warmed up. When planting peppers, make sure to give them space at one foot apart. Using mulch helps in retaining soil moisture. Reduces the need for watering especially during hot and dry periods.

- **Lettuce**
  Lettuce, a cool season vegetable, thrives in soil with a pH range of 6.0 to 7.0 that is loose and well drained. You have the option of either sowing lettuce seeds into the garden or starting them indoors and then moving them outside when appropriate. It's crucial to maintain moisture in the soil through watering.

- **Carrots**
  Carrots are root vegetables that thrive when exposed to sun but are best grown during months. The ideal pH for carrot growing soil ranges from around 6.0) to neutral (7.0). Directly sowing carrot seeds into the garden is recommended with a spacing of two inches, between each seedling. Once carrot seeds have germinated regular watering must be provided to prevent root drying.

- **Spinach**
  Spinach, a green vegetable is best grown in shade and can be harvested during the cold season. It prefers soil with an acidic, to pH (around 6.0 7.5) that is enriched with organic matter. You pant spinach seeds outdoors or start them indoors and later transfer them to the garden. To ensure its growth it requires watered soil that doesn't dry out easily so regular watering is essential. You have the option to harvest either the leaves or the entire plant when it's ready.

- **Beans**
  Beans, whether bush or pole varieties are warm season plants that thrive when exposed to sunlight. They prefer acidic to neutral soil (pH 6.0 7.0) that drains well. Once the soil has warmed up sufficiently you can directly plant beans in your garden space. It's important to consistently water beans during their flowering and pod forming stages.

- **Radishes**
  Radishes are root vegetables that flourish in sun they can also tolerate partial shade conditions. They grow best in soil with an acidic, to neutral pH range (around 6.0 7.0) and should be planted in well drained areas of your garden bed or container space ensuring proper drainage of excess water from the roots by using suitable containers or raised beds if necessary. Radishes grow quickly. Need watering, for healthy root development. Once they have reached the desired size you can start harvesting them.

- **Zucchini**

  For zucchini plants to thrive they require sunlight during the growing months. It's best to plant them in acidic to soil (pH 6.0 7.0) with good drainage. You can choose to sow zucchini seeds either indoors before transplanting them to the garden. Make sure to space them three to four feet. Keep the soil consistently moist by watering the plants. When the fruits reach a length of 6 8 inches they are ready for picking.

- **Onions**

  Onions are cool-season vegetables that prefer full sun exposure. They do well in soil that's slightly acidic to neutral (pH 6.0 7.0) and drains effectively. The spacing for planting onions varies depending on the variety whether planted from seeds or sets (bulbs). It's important to water them once or twice a week for an extended period of time. The time for harvesting is indicated when the leaves turn yellow and fall over

Planting Schedules and Optimal Spacing for Various Vegetables

Let's discuss the timing for planting vegetables and the spacing requirements between them. By managing the growth of plants we can make t the most of space, enhance their visual appeal and reduce maintenance efforts. Allow me to explain each aspect further;

Determining Planting Timetables

The ideal time to plant vegetables depends on your climate zone and the specific needs of each plant. Factors such as the frost date, average temperatures and daylight duration play a role in deciding when to sow seeds or transplant seedlings. It's important to follow these guidelines when preparing vegetable varieties.

a) **Cool Season Vegetables**; These types thrive in cooler climates. They include lettuce, spinach, kale, radishes, peas, broccoli among others. The best time to sow these vegetables is either during spring or late fall.

b) **Warm Season Vegetables**; These varieties prefer warmer climates Examples include tomatoes, peppers, cucumbers, beans, corn, squash and so on. It's crucial to wait until the risk of frost has passed before planting them in your area.

c) **Year Round Vegetables**; In temperate regions or with the use of season extenders like greenhouses or row covers, certain vegetables can be planted at any time throughout the year.

By considering these guidelines, for planting schedules and adapting them based on your location and climate conditions, you'll be able to optimize your vegetable gardens productivity while ensuring growth.

Carrots, beets, various herbs and different types of lettuce serve as examples of vegetables in this category. To determine the planting time, for items in your garden it's advisable to consult a local gardening guidebook, seek advice.

Spacing Requirements

Next, ensure that your plants have space between them to foster growth and maximize harvest success. By providing spacing each plant can receive water, sunlight and nutrients without competing with neighboring plants. This practice also helps slow down the spread of diseases and reduces resource competition Here are some factors to consider when determining the spacing;

a) **Seed Spacing**; When planting seeds directly in the ground carefully follow the instructions provided on the seed packets. This will prevent overcrowding. Promote growth for delicate seedlings. When starting seeds indoors or purchasing transplants it is important to adhere to recommended spacing guidelines based on the anticipated size of each plant at maturity. You can find this information on plant tags or seed packets. Make sure to allocate room for root expansion when transplanting

b) **Row Spacing**; Depending on the size of the vegetables you are growing you may need to adjust the distance between rows. The spacing between rows should be modified based on the dimensions of each vegetable variety. Tomatoes and peppers are examples of plants that require space between rows. When it comes to planting lettuce and radishes a spacing of 12-18 inches may be sufficient.

c) **Plant Spacing**; When it comes to row spacing it is important to consider the mature size and growth pattern of each plant. For vegetables like tomatoes it is recommended to provide three to four feet of space between plants. On the other hand, smaller leafy greens like lettuce may only require four to six inches. Certain plants such as pole beans and vining cucumbers also need space. To make the most of your growing area you can support these plants using trellises, pegs or cages.

Remember that each vegetable has its requirements and growth patterns. It is also important to consider companion planting. Providing room for your plants will ensure their growth.

To achieve success in vegetable gardening it is crucial to be aware of planting times and recommended distances between rows. Optimizing growing conditions by planting at the right times and providing enough space will prevent overcrowding, promote airflow, and maximize exposure to sunlight.

Providing Appropriate Support Structures for Climbing Plants

Providing appropriate Support structures for climbing plants are essential for their growth, productivity, and overall health. Climbing vegetables such as beans, peas, and cucumbers have a natural tendency to climb and require support to ensure their vines have something to cling to as they grow. Here, we will discuss the needs of climbing plants and various techniques to provide them with sturdy support structures.

1. **Understanding the needs of climbing vegetables**:

    a. **Vertical growth**: Climbing plants have a vining habit and tend to grow vertically rather than spreading horizontally like bush-type plants. They require support structures to guide their growth upwards.

    b. **Clinging mechanisms**: Climbing vegetables use different mechanisms to climb. Some varieties have tendrils that wrap around support structures, while others have twining stems that coil around them. Understanding the natural climbing behavior of each plant helps in providing suitable support.

    c. **Air circulation**: Adequate air circulation is crucial to prevent diseases and promote healthy growth. Providing appropriate support structures ensures that the plants are well-spaced and have good airflow around their foliage.

    d. Access to sunlight: Climbing plants need access to sunlight for photosynthesis and fruiting. Proper support structures help to position the plants optimally to receive adequate sunlight.

2. **Sturdy support structures**:

    a. Trellises: Trellises are vertical structures made of wood, bamboo, metal, or wire mesh. They consist of a framework of horizontal and vertical supports that provide a sturdy structure for the plants to climb on. Trellises can be freestanding or attached to walls or fences.

    b. Stakes: These are individual supports made of wood or metal that are inserted into the ground near the plants They are particularly useful for plants with a single main stem, such as tomatoes. The plant is tied to the stake as it grows, providing support and preventing it from falling over.

    c. Cages: Cages are large, robust structures made of wire mesh or metal, suitable for supporting plants. They provide 360-degree support to the plant and are ideal for sprawling varieties or plants with heavy fruits. Cages can be set up at the time of planting or added later as the plants grow.

3. **Training and guiding climbing plants**:

    a. **Tying**: As the plants grow, gently tie the vines to the support structure using soft garden twine or plant ties. Avoid using materials that can damage the plants or restrict their growth. Make loose knots to allow for expansion as the stems thicken.

    b. **Pruning and pinching**: Remove any lateral shoots or side branches that are not needed for upward growth. Pruning helps to maximize growth towards the main stem.

c. **Coiling and weaving**: For plants with twining stems, gently guide the main stem around the support structure, encouraging it to coil and weave its way upward. Monitor the growth regularly and make adjustments as necessary.
d. **Tendrils and hooks**: Plants with tendrils can be trained by gently wrapping the tendrils around the support structure or guiding them towards it. This will provide the tendrils with the necessary grip to stay attached.
e. **Regular maintenance**: Keep an eye on the plants as they grow, and make adjustments to the support structures as needed Ensure that the ties are secure but not too tight to avoid damaging the plants.

This not only maximizes your garden space but also promotes healthier plants, better airflow, and easier harvesting.

Pruning, Staking, and Training Techniques to Maximize Productivity

Pruning for Plant Health and Yields

Pruning plays a role, in gardening and farming as it enhances plant health and yields. This process involves removing leaves stems or branches from a plant. When done correctly pruning can boost fruit production improve plant well being and control growth. Now lets delve into the art of pruning and learn how to do it to maximize your efforts.

Enhancing Airflow and Ligh Exposure

An important function of pruning is to enhance airflow within plants, which's vital for their health. Dense foliage can restrict ventilation leading to increased humidity and higher susceptibility to diseases. By trimming branches and foliage we can improve air circulation and reduce the chances of fungal or bacterial infections. Furthermore by allowing light to reach the parts of the plant through pruning we stimulate photosynthesis and encourage healthy growth.

Optimizing Fruit Development

For fruit trees and flowering plants trimming is generally recommended for optimal fruit development. By cutting off branches at intervals through a technique called "thinning " we redirect the plants resources, towards fruit production. Thinning involves removing overcrowded branches so that the remaining ones can receive nutrients and bear larger fruits of better quality. Another advantage of thinning is preventing tree collapse caused by fruit weight.

Managing Plant Size and Shape

Pruning is a technique, for managing the size and shape of plants. When shrubs, hedges or ornamental trees are left to grow they can eventually outgrow their designated spaces. To maintain the desired height and form it's important to trim the branch tips or consider extensive methods like "rejuvenation pruning." By managing plant size you can maximize space efficiency enhance appeal and reduce maintenance efforts.

Here are some proven pruning techniques;

1. **Timing matters**; Pruning is most effective when done during the plants growth phase. It's crucial to understand the needs of each species and prune accordingly at the time.
2. **Use tools**; Keep your hand pruners, loppers and pruning saws sharp and clean. Using dirty tools can harm plants. Spread diseases. Remember to wipe down your tools after use and give them a rinse before storing them away.
3. **Educate yourself**; Successful tree trimming relies, on knowledge and practical application of techniques.

By following these guidelines you'll be able to prune your plants while promoting their growth without triggering any damage or stress caused by improper timing or tool usage. To maintain the health of plants various pruning techniques can be used such as heading cuts, thinning cuts and pinching. Each method has its contexts and purposes.

Consider the Plant's Well-being

When pruning it is crucial to consider the well being of the plant. Look out for signs of illness, injury or dead wood. Remove these areas to improve the plants health and prevent disease spread. Properly disposing of the trimmed materials is important to avoid any disease transmission. Additionally seeking advice, from gardeners can be beneficial if you are dedicated to becoming a vegetable gardener. Their insights can help you grow your vegetables successfully.

Staking and Training Techniques

Staking and training methods play a role in supporting fruiting plants ensuring they remain upright and increasing their yield. These practices contribute to maintaining erect plants of bearing the weight of their fruits. Lets explore some techniques for staking and training;

1. **Stakes with Knots**; One common technique involves using stakes with knots to support heavy plants, like tomatoes and peppers. The main stem can be securely tied to the stake using soft plant ties or twine. To ensure the stability and healthy growth of plants it's important to secure a stake, near the plant and periodically tie it as the plant grows. This helps prevent any toppling over and evenly distributes the weight of the fruit along the stem.

2. **Cages for Tomatoes**; Another method commonly used to support fruiting plants tomatoes is using cages. When the plant is still young place it within a wire cage that allows room for expansion. Guide its growth through the openings in the cage as it matures. This approach provides support prevents sprawling and keeps fruits and leaves off the ground reducing the risk of diseases and pests.

3. **Espalier for Fruit Trees**; For fruit trees like apples and pears espalier is a technique that optimizes yield while using space. It involves pruning and training branches to grow in a line against a surface such as a wall or trellis. By shaping these branches and securing them fruitful growth can be encouraged while maintaining an organized tree structure.

4. **Trellising for Climbing Plants**; Trellises are structures made with stakes or posts connected by supports. Utilizing espalier as a trellising method not increases production. Also adds an aesthetically pleasing display, to your garden. Certain climbing plants, including cucumbers, beans and grapes can greatly benefit from this method. Soft ties or twine are used to guide the vines as they grow and climb the trellis. This technique prevents the plants from toppling over. Ensures that the weight of the fruit is evenly distributed along their stems. Additionally trellising has advantages. It allows for an use of space and keeps the fruits off the ground where they could spoil.

Pruning and Pinching for Increased Yields

To maintain an optimal plant form and increase yields it's important to practice pruning and pinching techniques. Regularly remove any diseased branches to encourage the plant to focus its resources, on fruit development. Pinching is a method that encourages side branches to grow resulting in plants. This technique is commonly employed with basil and certain types of peppers to improve both branching and yields.

Supporting Heavy Fruits

In cases where heavy fruiters at risk of falling off and getting damaged using netting or support structures can be highly beneficial. This is particularly true for melons. Squash varieties. You can utilize a net or a cloth sling to support growing fruits or opt for systems, like hammocks. These structures help redistribute the weight of the fruit thereby reducing strain on the plant. When it comes to staking and training your plants it's important to consider their species, the size and weight of their fruits and how they individually grow. Additionally maintaining plant hygiene regularly monitoring them and making adjustments to ties or supports are essential, for a successful outcome. By staking and training your fruiting plants you can optimize your harvest. Enjoy a satisfying gardening experience, with healthy, upright and productive plants.

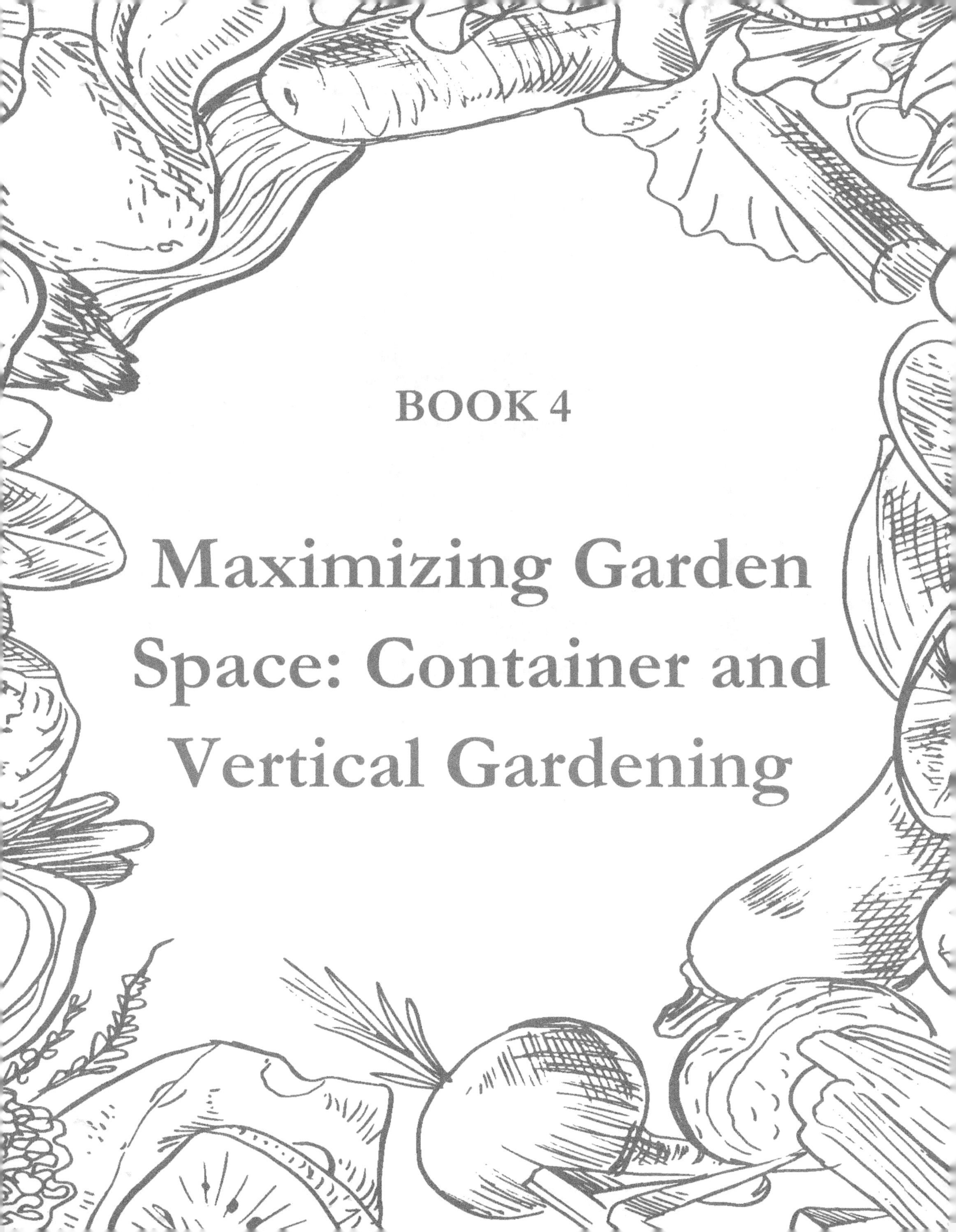

BOOK 4

Maximizing Garden Space: Container and Vertical Gardening

Book 4: Maximizing Garden Space: Container and Vertical Gardening

Introduction

Gardening is a popular hobby for many people, but not everyone has access to a large outdoor space to cultivate a traditional garden. Fortunately, there are innovative techniques that allow gardeners to maximize their available space by utilizing containers and vertical gardening. Growing plants in containers offers a wide variety of opportunities, regardless of whether you have a large yard, a balcony, a patio, or even just space within your home. In addition, the visual appeal of vibrant flowers or lush greenery may make your outdoor living space seem cozier and more inviting.

1. **Overcoming Space Limitations**: One of the primary reasons for embracing container and vertical gardening is the ability to overcome space limitations. Urban dwellers, apartment renters, or individuals with small yards can still enjoy the benefits of gardening by utilizing containers or vertical structures. These techniques allow gardening enthusiasts to make the most of their available space, whether it's a balcony, patio, or even a small indoor area.

2. **Accessibility for All**: Container and vertical gardening also provide accessibility for individuals with physical limitations or disabilities. Traditional gardening may require bending, kneeling, or other physically demanding tasks that can be challenging for some people. With container gardening, plants are raised to

a more accessible height, reducing strain on the back and knees. Vertical gardens can also be designed at a suitable height, enabling gardeners to tend to their plants comfortably without having to navigate uneven ground or large areas.

3. **Versatility in Plant Choices**: Both container and vertical gardening offer a wide range of plant choices. Almost any plant that can be grown in traditional gardens can also be grown in containers, including flowers, herbs, vegetables, and even small trees. Vertical gardening provides an opportunity to grow vining plants, such as tomatoes, cucumbers, beans, or climbing flowers. This versatility allows gardeners to tailor their gardens to their preferences and grow a diverse array of plants in a small space.

4. **Aesthetically Pleasing Designs**: Container and vertical gardens are not only functional but also aesthetically pleasing. They can be designed to add beauty and greenery to any space. Containers come in various sizes, shapes, and materials, allowing for creativity in designing visually appealing arrangements. Vertical structures, such as living walls or trellises, can create stunning focal points and transform bare walls or fences into living artworks. The combination of different plants and containers in a vertical garden can result in a visually striking display.

5. **Flexibility and Mobility**: Container gardening offers the advantage of flexibility and mobility. Containers can be easily rearranged to change the garden layout, adapt to seasonal sunlight variations, or simply satisfy the gardener's aesthetic preferences. This flexibility also allows gardeners to protect plants from extreme weather conditions or pests by relocating containers to more suitable locations. In addition, container gardens can be moved indoors during colder months, extending the growing season and enabling year-round gardening.

6. **Environmental Benefits**: Maximizing garden space through container and vertical gardening has environmental benefits as well. These techniques promote efficient use of resources such as water, soil, and fertilizers. Container gardens require less water compared to traditional gardens, as water can be precisely delivered to individual plants without wastage. Vertical gardens, with their compact design, minimize soil erosion and promote efficient nutrient uptake. Furthermore, the use of organic fertilizers and composting in container and vertical gardens can contribute to sustainable gardening practices.

Maximizing garden space through container and vertical gardening offers a practical and creative solution for individuals with limited space or physical limitations. These methods provide accessibility, versatility, and aesthetic appeal while promoting resource efficiency and environmental sustainability. Whether it's a small balcony, urban rooftop, or indoor setting, container and vertical gardening allow everyone to enjoy the joys of gardening and cultivate a thriving green oasis.

Exploring the Possibilities of Container Gardening for Small Spaces

If you're interested, in enjoying the benefits of growing your vegetables and plants but lack a plot of land, container gardening is an excellent choice. It offers possibilities for individuals with outdoor or indoor space.

In this discussion we'll explore the ways in which container gardening can help maximize the potential of an outdoor area:

1. **Flexibility and Space Optimization**
   First and foremost container gardening provides adaptability and practicality. While traditional pots and planters are perfectly suitable you can also utilize hanging baskets, window boxes or repurposed items like buckets, barrels or old furniture. This flexibility allows containers to be positioned horizontally on a windowsill or balcony railing or on a wall or trellis depending on the space.

2. **Accessibility and Mobility**
   Container gardening is particularly advantageous for those who have yards or no yard at all. By opting to grow plants in pots instead of in the ground, you can optimize your space usage. Every inch becomes valuable as you cultivate an array of fruits, vegetables, herbs and flowers, within containers.

   One way to assist individuals, with mobility issues is by placing containers on tables, shelves or raised platforms to reduce the need for bending or kneeling. Additionally you can transform your balcony or patio into a garden by growing plants in containers, which works well for spaces. Utilizing hanging baskets or wall-mounted containers not only maximizes space but also adds a visual appeal to your outdoor living area. For gardening enthusiasts container gardening is not limited to areas only; it can be done indoors as well. This allows year round gardening regardless of the weather. Is particularly useful for apartment dwellers or those without access to spaces. You can grow herbs like basil, mint and chives on windowsills using grow lights while fruiting plants such as strawberries and dwarf citrus trees thrive in an environment with appropriate conditions. Lastly container gardening offers the advantage of portability and easy accessibility due, to its mobility factor.

   Plants have the ability to be easily moved around in containers. This allows us to optimize their exposure to sunlight, protect them from weather conditions, or simply rearrange them for aesthetic purposes. This adaptability is particularly useful in environments where seasonal changes or space utilization shifts are common. Moreover container gardening can be beneficial for individuals with mobility issues as it allows them to set the pots at a height.

3. **Control over Soil Quality and Pest Management**
   When planting in containers instead of the ground, we have control over soil quality and can manage pests more effectively. To give our plants the chance of thriving its recommended to choose a mix that has been enriched with compost or other organic matter. When grown in containers plants are less susceptible to soil borne diseases. Weed infestation. By raising containers off the ground or utilizing natural pest management methods we can also control snails and slugs easily.

4. **Portability and Adaptability**
   Container gardening is not only a way to exercise our green thumbs but also allows us to enjoy all the benefits of gardening, even if we have limited outdoor space like a small yard, balcony, patio, or even an apartment. With some thinking, planning and selecting appropriate containers and plants we can create a beautiful and fruitful garden that perfectly fits our confined space.

Types of Containers for Container Gardening

There are types of containers commonly used for gardening.

1. **Pots and Planters**; The popular ones include pots and planters which come in different shapes sizes and materials, like clay, terracotta, ceramic or plastic. It's best to choose containers that allow water to drain easily such as those with holes at the bottom.

2. **Hanging Baskets**; For gardening hanging baskets are an option. They can be hung from hooks or brackets. Often have wire or plastic frames with coconut fiber liners or moss bottoms to hold the soil in place. Make sure these baskets have drainage holes and consider using a saucer or tray underneath to catch any water.

3. **Window Boxes**; Another option is window boxes, which're planters that can be attached to windowsills or balcony railings. They come in materials like plastic, metal or wood. To ensure they can support the weight of plants and soil use brackets or supports when installing them.

4. **Grow Bags**; Grow bags are another alternative made of cloth material. These permeable containers are great for growing vegetables, herbs and small plants as they provide airflow while preventing excessive moisture buildup inside. Opt for grow bags with handles, for portability.

5. **Vertical Planters**; Vertical planters offer an space saving solution, for growing plants in an orientation. These structures come with compartments or pockets to accommodate plants and can either stand freely or be mounted on walls. It's important to ensure that each pocket has drainage.

6. **Reusing Containers**; When it comes to reusing plastic bottles for storage options like buckets, barrels, tin cans or discarded furniture pieces can serve the purpose well. However before planting anything in these containers it's crucial to drill holes at the bottom for drainage.

Choosing the Right Soil Mix

For soil compositions in container gardening, it's recommended to use premium potting soil specifically designed for this purpose. Relying solely on garden soil may not provide sufficient drainage. Potting mixes are lightweight and drain well; they typically consist of ingredients like peat moss, perlite, vermiculite and organic matter.

Soilless Mixes

Soilless mixes, made from materials like peat or coco coir, are also commonly used These blends excel in terms of drainage, moisture retention and air circulation. They are easy to transport and help prevent infections that could be acquired from soil.

DIY Soil Mix

Alternatively you can create your soil mix by combining portions of peat moss, perlite or vermiculite and compost or well-rotted manure if you prefer a DIY approach.
This soil mixture offers drainage the ability to hold water effectively and a high concentration of nutrients.

Tips for Achieving Proper Drainage

1. Ensure your containers have drainage holes at the bottom. These openings allow excess water to escape, preventing the roots from drowning or decaying. If your containers don't already have holes you can create them by drilling or puncturing.
2. Place a saucer or tray beneath your containers to catch any leaking water. This helps avoid accumulation of water on indoor surfaces. Remember to empty the saucers to keep them dry.
3. Elevate your containers using pot feet or bricks for airflow and drainage by raising them off the ground.

Additionally it's crucial to use a mix that promotes water percolation through the soil and allows it to drain effectively from the container.

Watering Tips

To prevent root rot, avoid overwatering your pots. Check the moisture level of the soil by inserting your finger about an inch into it. If it feels dry, it's time to water. If it's still damp, you can wait a bit longer before watering again.

Creating an Environment for Plant Growth

To ensure that your plants thrive in container gardening it's important to create an environment, for their growth. This can be achieved by selecting containers using the soil mixes and ensuring proper drainage procedures are, in place.

Techniques for Growing Vegetables in Limited Areas

Growing vegetables in limited areas can be a challenging task, but with innovative techniques and strategies, it is possible to maximize space and yield a bountiful harvest.

Here are some techniques commonly used for growing vegetables in confined spaces:

1. **Raised Beds**: Raised beds are a popular choice for small gardens or areas with limited soil. They are essentially elevated planting areas created by constructing a frame and filling it with high-quality soil mix. Raised beds offer several advantages, including improved drainage, better soil quality control, reduced weed competition, and ease of access. Vegetables can be grown in close proximity, optimizing space utilization.

2. **Container Gardening**: Container gardening involves growing vegetables in pots, containers, or other suitable vessels. This technique is ideal for small balconies, patios, or even indoor spaces. Vegetables like tomatoes, peppers, lettuce, herbs, and radishes can thrive in containers. Use lightweight, well-draining potting soil, and ensure containers have proper drainage holes. Vertical stacking or tiered containers can further maximize space utilization.

3. **Hanging Baskets**: Hanging baskets are an effective way to utilize vertical space for vegetable cultivation. Options include traditional hanging baskets or specially designed vertical planters. Vegetables with trailing or cascading growth habits, such as cherry tomatoes, strawberries, and trailing herbs like thyme and oregano, work well in hanging baskets. Ensure adequate support and drainage for the baskets.

4. **Vertical Gardening**: Vertical gardening utilizes walls, trellises, or structures to grow vegetables vertically, thereby conserving horizontal space. Additionally, you can use specialized vertical planters or modular systems designed for vertical vegetable gardening.

5. **Intensive Planting and Succession Planting**: Intensive planting refers to growing vegetables in close proximity, optimizing every inch of available space. By utilizing techniques such as square foot gardening or interplanting compatible crops, you can maximize yields in limited areas. Succession planting involves planting crops in succession, allowing for continuous harvest throughout the growing season. As one crop is harvested, another is planted in its place, ensuring efficient use of space and a steady supply of fresh produce.

6. **Vertical Hydroponics and Aeroponics**: Hydroponics and aeroponics are soilless cultivation techniques that can be adapted for use in vertical gardening. Vertical hydroponic towers or aeroponic systems allow for the growth of a large number of plants in a compact space, making them suitable for urban farming or indoor gardening.

7. **Microgreen and Sprout Cultivation**: Microgreens and sprouts are young, tender vegetable shoots that can be grown in small trays or containers indoors. These crops have a quick growth cycle and can be harvested within a few weeks. Microgreens are typically grown from the seeds of vegetables like lettuce,

kale, radishes, and herbs. Sprouts are grown from seeds like mung beans, alfalfa, broccoli, and lentils. They require minimal space and provide a nutrient-dense harvest.

8. **Vertical Herb Gardens**: Growing vegetables in confined spaces can be challenging; however, with creative methods and strategies, you can maximize the available space and yield a plentiful crop. Herbs like basil, parsley, cilantro, and mint can thrive in vertical arrangements.

When employing these techniques, it's important to consider factors such as sunlight exposure, watering requirements, proper soil preparation, and regular maintenance to ensure healthy plant growth. Additionally, choosing suitable vegetable varieties that are well-suited for container or vertical cultivation will contribute to successful gardening in limited areas.

Selecting compact and dwarf varieties of vegetables is crucial when growing in smaller spaces. These varieties are specifically bred to have smaller growth habits, making them ideal for containers, raised beds, and vertical gardens.

Here are some tips on how to select and choose the right compact and dwarf varieties for a bountiful harvest in limited spaces:

1. **Research and Seed Catalogs**: Start by researching compact and dwarf vegetable varieties. Many seed companies provide specific categories or sections in their catalogs dedicated to these varieties. Look for terms like "compact," "dwarf," "patio," or "bush" in the vegetable descriptions. Seed catalogs often provide valuable information on the growth habit, recommended container size, and yield potential of each variety.

2. **Size and Spacing**: Consider the mature size and spacing requirements of the plants. Look for varieties that have a smaller overall footprint and can be planted closer together. Compact and dwarf varieties typically have shorter stems, smaller leaves, and a more bushy growth habit. This allows for denser planting and efficient space utilization.

3. **Yield and Production**: While compact varieties may have smaller overall plants, they can still provide a bountiful harvest. Look for varieties that are known for their high productivity and continuous fruiting or harvesting. Some compact varieties are specifically bred to have higher yields to compensate for their smaller size. Consider the expected yield per plant or per square foot when making your selection.

4. **Suitability for Containers**: Ensure that the compact or dwarf varieties are suitable for container gardening. Look for varieties that are specifically recommended for pots or containers. These varieties usually have shallow root systems, making them well-suited for limited soil volumes. Also, check the recommended container size for each variety to ensure it fits within your available space.

5. **Disease Resistance**: Disease resistance is crucial in any garden, but it becomes even more important in small spaces where diseases can spread easily. Look for compact and dwarf varieties that have good disease

resistance or tolerance to common pests and diseases. Disease-resistant varieties will reduce the risk of crop loss and minimize the need for chemical interventions.

6. **Crop Preference**: Consider your personal preferences and the vegetables you enjoy eating. Focus on selecting compact or dwarf varieties of the vegetables that you and your family love to eat. This ensures that you get the most value and enjoyment from your limited garden space.

7. **Vertical Growing Habits**: Some compact and dwarf varieties have natural vertical or upright growth habits, which make them suitable for trellising or vertical gardening. These plants can be trained to grow vertically, maximizing space utilization and enhancing the aesthetic appeal of your garden.

8. **Climate Adaptation**: Choose compact and dwarf varieties that are well-adapted to your specific climate and growing conditions. Consider factors such as temperature tolerance, day length requirements, and overall suitability for your region. This will increase the chances of successful growth and a bountiful harvest.

Remember to follow proper care and maintenance practices, including adequate watering, fertilizing, and pest management, to ensure the healthy growth and productivity of your compact and dwarf vegetable plants.

Vertical Gardening Solutions for Maximizing Yield in Tight Spaces

Vertical gardening is an innovative and efficient solution for maximizing yield in tight spaces. I It involves utilizing vertical surfaces such as walls, fences, or trellises to grow vegetables upward, thus optimizing space utilization This method is particularly useful in urban areas or small gardens where horizontal space is limited. By employing vertical gardening techniques, you can unlock the potential of your available space and cultivate a variety of crops.

Here are some key aspects and solutions to consider when implementing vertical gardening for maximizing yield in tight spaces:

1. **Selection of Suitable Plants**: Choose plants that are well-suited for vertical growth and have a compact or vining growth habit. Some ideal options include vine tomatoes, cucumbers, beans, peas, lettuce, herbs, strawberries, and certain varieties of peppers. These plants can climb, sprawl, or trail upwards, making them perfect candidates for vertical gardening.

2. **Structural Support**: Create a sturdy and reliable support structure to facilitate vertical growth. This can be achieved through the installation of trellises, arbors, stakes, or hanging baskets. Ensure that the structure is securely anchored to the ground or walls to withstand the weight of the plants and withstand environmental conditions.

3. **Wall-Mounted Solutions**: Attach planter boxes, pockets, or containers directly to walls or fences. These can be made of various materials such as wood, metal, or plastic. Ensure that the materials are durable, water-resistant, and allow proper drainage. This method maximizes the use of vertical space and can be particularly effective for herbs, lettuces, and trailing plants.

4. **Hanging Baskets**: Hang baskets from a sturdy support system, such as hooks or overhead frames. Hanging baskets are versatile and can be used for growing a wide range of plants, including trailing vines and compact vegetables. They are especially useful for areas with limited ground space.

5. **Modular Vertical Systems**: Consider utilizing modular vertical gardening systems, which consist of stackable containers or panels that can be easily mounted on walls or stacked on top of one another. These systems often feature integrated irrigation and drainage systems for convenient watering and maintenance. They provide flexibility in terms of adjusting the layout and can be easily expanded as needed.

6. **Living Walls or Green Walls**: Living walls are vertical structures covered with vegetation, creating a visually appealing and productive garden space. These walls can be constructed using a variety of materials, including pockets, trays, or specialized planters that hold the soil and plants. Living walls often incorporate an irrigation system to ensure proper hydration for the plants.

7. **Espalier Technique**: Espalier is a pruning and training technique that involves training fruit trees, such as apple or pear trees, along a flat plane, such as a wall or fence. This technique allows the tree to grow horizontally while maximizing fruit production. Espaliered trees require regular pruning and support to maintain their desired shape.

8. **Intensive Planting and Succession Planting**: Maximize yield by employing intensive planting techniques, such as intercropping and companion planting. These methods involve planting crops in close proximity to optimize space utilization and reduce competition for resources. Additionally, practice succession planting by planting new crops as soon as previous ones are harvested to ensure a continuous supply of fresh produce throughout the growing season.

9. **Adequate Lighting and Watering**: Ensure that your vertical garden receives sufficient light and water. Position the garden in an area that receives optimal sunlight based on the plant's requirements. Consider using artificial lighting, such as grow lights, for indoor or shaded vertical gardens. Implement an efficient watering system, such as drip irrigation or self-watering containers, to ensure plants receive the necessary moisture without wasting water.

10. **Soil and Nutrient Considerations**: Select a high-quality soil mix that provides adequate drainage and nutrient retention. Vertical gardens often require lightweight soil blends to prevent excessive weight on the structures. Additionally, incorporate organic matter and compost to improve soil fertility and enhance plant growth.

By implementing these vertical gardening solutions, you can effectively maximize yield in tight spaces while creating a visually appealing and productive garden. Remember to consider the specific needs of your chosen plants and adapt the solutions accordingly to ensure optimal growth and harvest.

Vertical gardening systems offer diverse options for maximizing yield and creating visually stunning gardens. Let's explore some popular systems, including vertical towers, living walls, and hydroponic setups:

1. **Vertical Towers**: Vertical towers, also known as vertical planters or vertical gardening systems, are self-contained structures that allow plants to grow vertically. These towers typically consist of stacked trays or pockets, each containing a plant or multiple plants. Water and nutrients are often supplied through a recirculating system, ensuring efficient use of resources. Vertical towers are commonly used for growing small vegetables, herbs, and strawberries. They are space-efficient, easy to manage, and suitable for both indoor and outdoor environments.

2. **Living Walls**: Living walls, also referred to as green walls or vertical gardens, are vertical structures covered with vegetation. They can be installed indoors or outdoors, offering aesthetic appeal and numerous environmental benefits. Living walls can be created using various systems, such as modular panels, fabric pockets, or specialized planters attached to a wall or frame. These systems typically incorporate an irrigation system to supply water and nutrients to the plants. Living walls offer versatility in plant selection, allowing for a mix of ornamental plants, herbs, and even edible crops. They enhance air quality, reduce noise levels, and provide insulation.

3. **Hydroponic Systems**: Hydroponic systems are soilless gardening systems that utilize water-based nutrient solutions to cultivate plants. In vertical hydroponics, plants are often arranged in stacked layers or columns, with their roots suspended in a nutrient-rich solution. Some hydroponic systems utilize

techniques like nutrient film technique (NFT), aeroponics, or vertical recirculating systems. These systems provide precise control over water, nutrients, and environmental conditions, leading to faster growth rates and higher yields. Hydroponics is particularly advantageous in vertical gardening as it maximizes space utilization, conserves water, and allows year-round cultivation.

4. **Aeroponics**: Aeroponics is a variation of hydroponics where plants are grown in an air or mist environment without the use of soil. The plant roots are suspended in air, and a fine mist or nutrient-rich solution is periodically sprayed onto the roots. Aeroponic systems provide excellent oxygenation to the roots, resulting in rapid growth and increased yields. In vertical gardening, aeroponic towers or columns can be utilized to cultivate a variety of crops, including leafy greens, herbs, and small vegetables.

5. **Tower Gardens**: Tower gardens are vertical aeroponic systems that enable the cultivation of a variety of plants in a compact space. They consist of tall vertical columns with multiple planting pockets or trays. The plants receive water and nutrients through a misting system, providing optimal moisture levels and nutrient uptake. Tower gardens are ideal for growing a wide range of crops, including lettuce, spinach, herbs, strawberries, and even larger plants like tomatoes and peppers. They are commonly used in both residential and commercial settings, such as restaurants and urban farms.

6. **Pocket Gardens**: Pocket gardens involve attaching fabric or felt pockets to a wall or frame, creating a vertical planting space. These pockets allow for planting a variety of plants, from flowers and herbs to vegetables. Pocket gardens are lightweight, flexible, and easy to install. They are often used to create decorative and functional vertical gardens in small spaces, balconies, or urban environments.

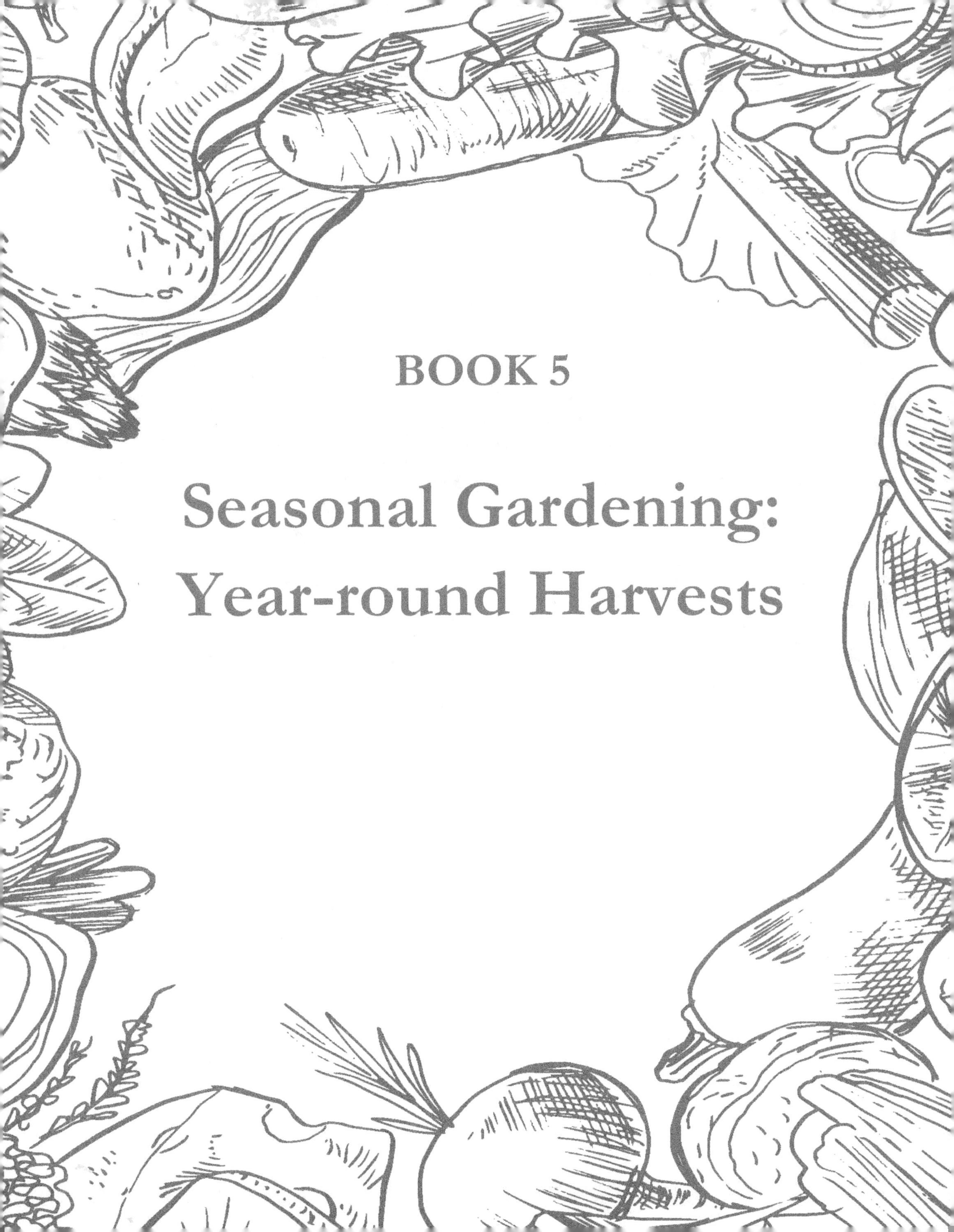

BOOK 5

Seasonal Gardening: Year-round Harvests

Book 5: Seasonal Gardening: Year-round Harvests

Introduction

Growing plants and harvests in accordance with the seasons' natural cycles is a traditional gardening approach. However, it is now feasible to prolong the growing season and produce crops all year round thanks to technological breakthroughs and improvements in gardening methods. The practice of "seasonal" or "year-round" gardening has grown in favor among gardeners and enthusiasts who wish to have access to fresh vegetables all year long.

Indoor Gardening Techniques

First, plants can survive in regulated surroundings independent of the weather outside thanks to the advent of indoor gardening techniques like hydroponics, vertical farming, and greenhouse production. These methods provide the ideal temperature, lighting, and fertilizer supply for growing plants, which promotes quicker development and larger harvests.

Artificial Lighting Systems for indoor Gardening

Furthermore, during the shorter and darker winter days, artificial lighting systems including high-intensity discharge lamps (HID), light-emitting diodes (LED), and fluorescent lights assist mimic the essential sunshine for plant development. These lighting systems can be adjusted for each stage of plant growth, to provide the appropriate spectrum and duration of light

Selection of Suitable Plant Varieties

The choice of the right plant kinds is essential for year-round gardening. Some plants are inherently better suited to longer growth seasons or enclosed spaces. Gardeners may maximize their harvests all through the year by selecting cultivars that are more tolerant to temperature changes, disease-resistant, or have shorter maturation periods. In response to consumer demand for year-round gardening, breeding programs and seed companies have developed new cultivars that are specially suited for extended growth seasons

Temperature Control Systems

Furthermore, the popularity of year-round gardening has been aided by the accessibility of cutting-edge temperature control systems. Accurate temperature and humidity management is made possible by sophisticated heating, ventilation, and air conditioning (HVAC) systems, which foster the best possible circumstances for plant development. Automated systems with sensors and timers assist in maintaining constant environmental parameters, which lowers the amount of human effort needed to monitor and modify the growth environment.

Benefits of Year-Round Gardening

Gardening all year round has several advantages for both people and society:

- **Consistent Supply of Fresh Vegetables**; First of all, it enables a consistent and continual supply of healthy, fresh vegetables regardless of seasonal restrictions. This can enhance food security, particularly in areas where access to fresh produce may be limited during certain times of the year . Additionally, it encourages independence and lessens reliance on imported food and long-distance travel.

- **Improved Sustainability**; Additionally, by lowering the carbon footprint associated with traditional agriculture, year-round gardening may improve sustainability. Local food production and a reduction in long-distance transportation can greatly decrease energy usage and greenhouse gas emissions Additionally, since water can be precisely managed and recirculated within, indoor gardening techniques use less water than conventional outside farming.

- **Educational and Recreational Value**; Additionally, gardening all year round offers educational and recreational advantages. It enables people to get first-hand knowledge of plant biology, agricultural techniques, and sustainable living. In addition to bringing individuals closer to nature and giving them a feeling of success as they see their plants flourish and generate food, gardening may also be soothing and fun.

Today, it is feasible to produce reliable and bountiful harvests all year long by combining innovative indoor gardening methods, artificial lighting systems, temperature control technology, and compatible plant kinds. This method encourages food security, sustainability, and individual well-being, making it a desirable choice for both people and communities.

Extending the Growing Season with Techniques like Cold Frames and Row Covers

For gardeners and farmers who wish to optimize their crop and enjoy fresh products for a longer length of time, extending the growing season is a useful strategy. Row covers and cold frames are two widely used techniques for extending the growing season, protecting plants from frost, and starting spring planting early. Let's examine these strategies in further depth.

1. **Cold Frames**: In essence, cold frames are closed enclosures with solid sides and translucent tops, usually constructed of glass or plastic. They are positioned directly on the ground and serve as little greenhouses, absorbing and holding solar heat. Here's how to construct and use cold frames effectively:

    - **Construction**: Wood, bricks, or cinder blocks are just a few of the materials that may be used to construct a cold frame. In order to optimize solar exposure and improve insulation, the clear top should be slanted. To avoid overheating on bright days, it's essential to make sure there is enough ventilation.
    - **Placement**: Pick a spot with plenty of sunshine exposure; ideally, it should be facing south. Avoid locations with a lot of shadow or wind. To guard against wind damage, the cold frame should be placed on flat ground and well fastened.
    - **Planting**: Due to its ability to provide a warmer microclimate, cold frames enable you to begin planting earlier in the spring. Several weeks before to the final day of frost, sow seeds or transfer seedlings into the cold frame. Young plants are shielded from the cold in the enclosed space, which helps them establish and develop more rapidly.
    - **Temperature control**: On warm days, the cold frame should be opened or ventilated to avoid overheating. To keep the heat in on chilly evenings, shut the frame. To guarantee ideal growth circumstances, it's crucial to keep an eye on the temperature within the cold frame.

2. **Row Covers**: Row covers are thin, partially transparent textiles or sheets that are draped directly over plants in order to provide a barrier of protection. They act as insulation and protect plants from wind, insects, and cold. Here's how to use row covers effectively:

    - **Material selection**: Row covers come in a variety of materials, including agricultural cloth, floating row cover fabric, and even used bedsheets. Based on your unique demands, choose a fabric with the proper thickness, which is often expressed in ounces per square yard. Lighter textiles enable greater sunlight access but provide less insulation.
    - **Installation**: Row coverings may be draped directly over plants or held up by wire or PVC pipe hoops or frames. To keep the cover from blowing away or moving during windstorms, it should be fastened at the edges. To enable room for plant development, leave some wiggle room in the cloth.
    - **Water and airflow**: In order to avoid excessive moisture accumulation and illness, make sure that row covers provide proper water penetration and ventilation. Watering may be carried out via the cloth or by momentarily raising it. On bright days, periodically raise or remove the coverings to provide pollinators access to the plants.

- **Seasonal adjustment**: Early spring and late autumn are both good times to utilize row covers. They enable early planting by shielding plants from spring frosts. By shielding plants from light frost and chilly temperatures in the autumn, row covers may lengthen the growth season and enable longer harvests.

Row covers and cold frames are both practical ways to lengthen the growing season and shield plants from frost. By using these methods, farmers and gardeners in even colder regions can start growing early in the spring and enjoy fresh produce for an extended period. To maximize the advantages and achieve good outcomes, try out several variations of these techniques and modify them according to your unique circumstances.

Advantages of Extending the Growing Season

Techniques for extending the growing season, such cold frames and row covers, provide a number of advantages for enhancing microclimates and extending the window for harvesting vegetables from your garden.

Here are some key advantages:

1. **Protection from frost**: Frost can impede the growth of delicate plants or even kill them, causing them to wither. Row covers and cold frames serve as barriers, protecting plants from frost by enclosing heat and warming the surrounding area. You may plant earlier in the spring and harvest far into the autumn thanks to this protection.

2. **Early planting**: You may start planting seeds or transferring seedlings earlier than the suggested outdoor planting dates by employing season extension strategies. Row covers and cold frames provide a warmer environment that enables faster germination and growth of plants. By doing this, you get a head start and extend the growth season.

3. **Heat retention**: Row covers and cold frames both catch and hold onto heat from sunshine, improving the environment for plants. They serve as insulation, halting the loss of heat during chilly nights. Particularly during transitional times when temperatures might change, this heat retention aids in maintaining ideal growth conditions.

4. **Increased growth rate**: Plants develop more quickly in the warmer and safer environment that season extension methods give. This enhanced growth rate can result in earlier and greater yields. Additionally, the prolonged growing season permits several crop successions, allowing for a continual harvest for a protracted period of time.

5. **Pest and critter control**: Techniques for extending the growing season provide a physical barrier against animals and pests, so limiting their access to your plants. Insects, birds, rabbits, and other small animals are kept away from your veggies in particular by row coverings. Damage is minimized and fewer chemical treatments are necessary thanks to this protection.
6. **Environmental control**: You have better control over the growing environment using cold frames and row coverings. You can control the humidity levels, airflow, and exposure to sunshine in these buildings

by regulating the ventilation and temperature. This control can help to mitigate adverse conditions and protect plants during periods of severe weather

7. **Crop diversification**: Using ways to extend the growing season, you may experiment with a larger variety of crops, including ones that are more suited to warmer regions. You may effectively cultivate heat-loving plants that might otherwise struggle in your area by establishing conducive microclimates. This variety expands your culinary possibilities and also yields a more diverse and plentiful crop

8. **Sustainable gardening**: You may lessen your dependency on off-season products sent from far-off places by using season extension strategies. By reducing food miles and related carbon emissions, this strategy encourages sustainable gardening practices. Additionally, it enables you to enjoy seasonal, fresh veggies produced at home, increasing self-sufficiency and minimizing your environmental impact.

The harvest window for your vegetable garden may be extended and ideal microclimates are created using season extension methods, which overall has several advantages. These methods boost production, expand crop variety, and encourage sustainable gardening methods by shielding plants from cold, enhancing growing conditions, and giving control over the environment.

Planting and Caring for Cool-Season and Warm-Season Crops

It's important to bear in mind the distinctions between planting and taking care of season and cool season crops when dealing with either type. By understanding these differences gardeners can make choices that enhance productivity and support growth. Now let's delve into the details

Cool Season Crops

Cool season crops are plants that thrive in cool climates Can tolerate light frosts. They typically prefer temperatures ranging from 40F (4C) to 70F (21C). These crops are usually sown in spring, summer or early fall when the temperatures are more favorable. Examples of cool season vegetables include lettuce, spinach, kale, broccoli, cauliflower, peas, carrots, radishes and beets.

Prepare the soil for growing cool season crops by removing weeds and incorporating resources, like compost. This will improve both soil drainage and fertility. Follow the instructions provided on the seed packet regarding seed depth and spacing while planting them. Take care to water the planted seeds thoroughly. Maintain a level of soil moisture throughout the planting and growing stages. If your seedlings are becoming overcrowded it's time to thin them out.

To maintain soil moisture and prevent weed growth it is beneficial to use mulch around the plants. For cool season crops it is ideal to harvest them once they have fully matured but before hot weather arrives.

Warm Season Crops

On the other hand, warm season crops thrive in temperatures ranging from 70 to 95 degrees Fahrenheit (21 to 35 degrees Celsius). These crops are typically planted in spring, after the risk of frost has passed and the soil has warmed up. Some examples of warm season crops that flourish during the months include tomatoes, peppers, cucumbers, zucchini, corn, beans, melons and squash.

Before planting warm season crops ensure that the soil is warm enough and easy to work with. Enhancing soil fertility and drainage can be achieved by incorporating organic matter While some warm season crops can be transplanted into the garden others can be directly sown into the soil. Pay attention to recommended planting depths and row spacing for growth. Once the plants roots establish themselves in the ground you can reduce watering frequency while ensuring adequate moisture levels are maintained. Using mulch around plants plays a role, in retaining soil moisture and preventing weed growth. As your vine crops grow larger and more sprawling, you may want to consider using stakes or trellises for support

Warm season crops typically reach their peak size, color or maturity during the middle of summer or the beginning of October. It is important to care for all crops throughout the year. This involves being vigilant, in monitoring and controlling pests and diseases as taking appropriate preventative measures. Adding compost and using fertilizers provides nutrients during the growing season. Regular weeding helps eliminate competition for resources and nutrients. To ensure air circulation and prevent disease spread it is advisable to maintain a distance between plants. Each crop has maintenance requirements, such as staking tomatoes or pruning plants that need to be met for optimal growth and yield.

By understanding the differences between cool season and warm season crops, as well as knowing the best times to plant and care for each type, gardeners can enjoy a plentiful harvest throughout the year.

Vegetables that Thrive in Both Warm and Cool Climates

Below are some vegetables that thrive in both warm climates along with suggestions on how to care for them to ensure a harvest;

1. **Spinach**; Spinach is a green that grows well in both warm regions. Plant spinach seeds during seasons such, as spring or late summer/fall. When planting it's important to use soil that's rich, in compost and well drained. To prevent bolting make sure the soil remains consistently moist and provide some shade during periods. It's also beneficial to remove the leaves to promote continued growth.

2. **Carrots**; Carrots are a root vegetable that can be grown in both warm climates. For sowing choose spring or late summer as ideal times. To encourage root development make sure the soil is loose and free of any objects. Keep the soil moist without overwatering. As carrots require space to grow you'll need to thin out the seedlings as they become larger. When the roots have reached their desired size, gently pull them from the ground.

3. **Lettuce**; Lettuce thrives in cooler weather and can be grown year round in shaded areas. Select varieties that can tolerate sunlight and heat for warm season gardens. Ensure that the soil is moist but well drained by watering it while avoiding saturation. Baby lettuce can be harvested either by cutting the plant or by picking leaves as needed.

4. **Radishes**; Radishes are a type of vegetable that can be grown in both warm regions. They have a growth rate so you can plant the seeds directly into drained soil during early spring, late summer or early fall. It's important to keep the soil consistently moist for root development and seed germination. Remember to thin out the seedlings to give them space to grow properly. Harvest the radishes at their size to avoid them developing skin if left to mature further.

5. **Cucumbers**; Next lets talk about cucumbers. These are warm season crops that require time in the soil. You can plant cucumber seeds. Use transplants after the last frost of April. To ensure growth choose a spot, with well drained soil enriched with compost. Make sure to water the soil especially while the fruits are developing. Vining cucumber plants will need support from trellises or cages. Harvest them when they are still crisp but not fully ripened for a supply.

6. **Beans**; Beans, whether bush beans or pole beans also thrive in sun during months. Sow bean seeds in soil once there is no danger of frost in springtime. For pole beans provide support like trellises or poles for their climbing nature. It's crucial to maintain moisture levels in the soil, throughout their flowering and pod growth stages. Beans will produce a yield of pods if they are harvested regularly while still young and tender.

7. **Tomatoes**; Tomatoes, ranked seventh on the list can be grown throughout the summer months as they require a growing season and ample sunlight. Start by planting seeds or transplants indoors after the frost, in April. Choose a location with drainage, sufficient organic matter and a pH level between 6.0 to 6.8. To provide support, for your tomato plants use stakes or cages. It is important to keep the soil moist through frequent watering. Applying mulch around the plants helps retain moisture and prevents weed growth. For flavor pick tomatoes when they are perfectly ripe.

Vegetables can thrive in both warm and cool climates When planning and caring for your crops it's essential to consider the conditions of your environment.

Harvesting and Storing Vegetables to Enjoy Fresh Produce throughout the Year

Harvesting and storing vegetables properly is an essential skill for anyone interested in enjoying fresh produce throughout the year. By learning the proper techniques and timing, you can ensure that your harvested vegetables maintain their peak flavor and nutritional value. Here are some key considerations:

1. **Timing**: Harvest vegetables at their peak maturity. Each vegetable has its own indicators of ripeness, such as color, size, and texture. Refer to seed packets, gardening books, or online resources to determine the optimal harvesting time for specific vegetables.

2. **Morning Harvest**: It's generally best to harvest vegetables in the morning when the temperatures are cooler. This helps preserve their freshness and nutritional content.

3. **Harvesting Techniques**:
    - **Use sharp, clean tools**: Utilize clean, sharp scissors, pruners, or garden knives to minimize damage to the plant and harvested produce.
    - **Handle with care**: Handle vegetables gently to avoid bruising or crushing them.
    - **Cut, snap, or twist**: Different vegetables require specific harvesting techniques. Some vegetables like tomatoes or cucumbers are typically harvested by gently twisting or snapping them off the vine, while others like lettuce or herbs can be cut with scissors or knives.

4. **Proper Storage**:
    - **Remove excess dirt**: Gently brush off any excess soil from harvested vegetables to prevent rot and decay.
    - **Sort and separate**: Sort vegetables by type and remove any damaged or diseased specimens. Separating them helps prevent spoilage from spreading.
    - **Temperature and humidity**: Most vegetables should be stored in cool and humid environments. However, some vegetables have specific temperature and humidity requirements. For example, leafy greens prefer cooler temperatures (around 32°F/0°C) with higher humidity, while root vegetables like carrots or potatoes prefer cooler temperatures (around 40-50°F/4-10°C) with lower humidity.
    - **Packaging**: Store vegetables in breathable containers like mesh bags, perforated plastic bags, or open containers to allow for air circulation. Avoid sealing vegetables in airtight bags, as this can lead to moisture buildup and spoilage.
    - **Avoid ethylene exposure**: Some fruits and vegetables, like tomatoes and apples, produce ethylene gas, which can cause premature ripening and spoilage in other produce. Keep ethylene-producing and ethylene-sensitive vegetables separated to maintain freshness.
    - **Location**: Store harvested vegetables in a cool, dark place, such as a root cellar, basement, or refrigerator, depending on the specific requirements of the vegetables.

5. **Monitoring**: Regularly check your stored vegetables for any signs of spoilage or decay. Remove any rotting vegetables immediately to prevent them from affecting others.

6. **Preservation Techniques**: If you want to enjoy your harvested vegetables for an extended period, consider various preservation methods such as canning, freezing, or dehydrating. These techniques can help you preserve the flavor and nutritional value of the vegetables.

Here are some popular methods of vegetable preservation that can help you enjoy your homegrown produce even during the off-season:

1. **Canning**:
   - Water bath canning: This method is suitable for high-acid vegetables like tomatoes, pickles, and fruits. The food is heated in jars submerged in boiling water to kill bacteria and create a vacuum seal.
   - Pressure canning: Recommended for low-acid vegetables like green beans, corn, and root vegetables. The food is placed in jars and processed under pressure to reach the required temperature for safe preservation.

2. **Freezing**:
   - Blanching: Many vegetables benefit from blanching before freezing. Briefly immerse them in boiling water, then transfer to an ice bath to halt the cooking process. Blanching helps retain color, texture, and nutritional value.
   - Flash freezing: Spread prepared vegetables in a single layer on a baking sheet and place them in the freezer. Once frozen, transfer them to airtight containers or freezer bags. This method prevents clumping and allows you to remove individual portions as needed.

3. **Drying**:
   - Air drying: Suitable for herbs, hot peppers, and some root vegetables. Hang the vegetables in a well-ventilated area with low humidity until they are completely dry.
   - Dehydrator: Use an electric dehydrator to remove moisture from vegetables at a controlled temperature. This method preserves the flavor and nutrients while extending shelf life.
   - Oven drying: Set your oven to a low temperature and spread sliced or chopped vegetables on a baking sheet. Leave the oven door slightly ajar to allow moisture to escape. This method works well for herbs, tomatoes, and some root vegetables.

4. **Fermenting**:
   - Fermentation involves using beneficial bacteria to preserve vegetables. Popular examples include sauerkraut, kimchi, and pickles. Fermented vegetables not only have extended shelf life but also offer probiotic benefits.

5. **Vacuum sealing**:
   - This method involves using a vacuum sealer to remove air from specially designed bags or containers. To destroy microorganisms and produce a vacuum seal, food is heated in jars, which are then immersed in boiling water. It is often used in conjunction with freezing or refrigeration.

6. **Root cellaring**:
    - If you have access to a cool and humid basement or root cellar, you can store certain root vegetables like carrots, beets, and potatoes in bins or boxes filled with sand, sawdust, or straw. The insulating material helps maintain a steady temperature and humidity level, extending their shelf life.

When using any preservation method, it's important to follow proper food safety guidelines, including using clean equipment, appropriate storage containers, and labeling the preserved vegetables with the date and contents.

Experiment with different preservation methods to find the ones that suit your preferences and the types of vegetables you grow. Each method offers unique advantages and can help you enjoy the flavors of homegrown produce all year round.

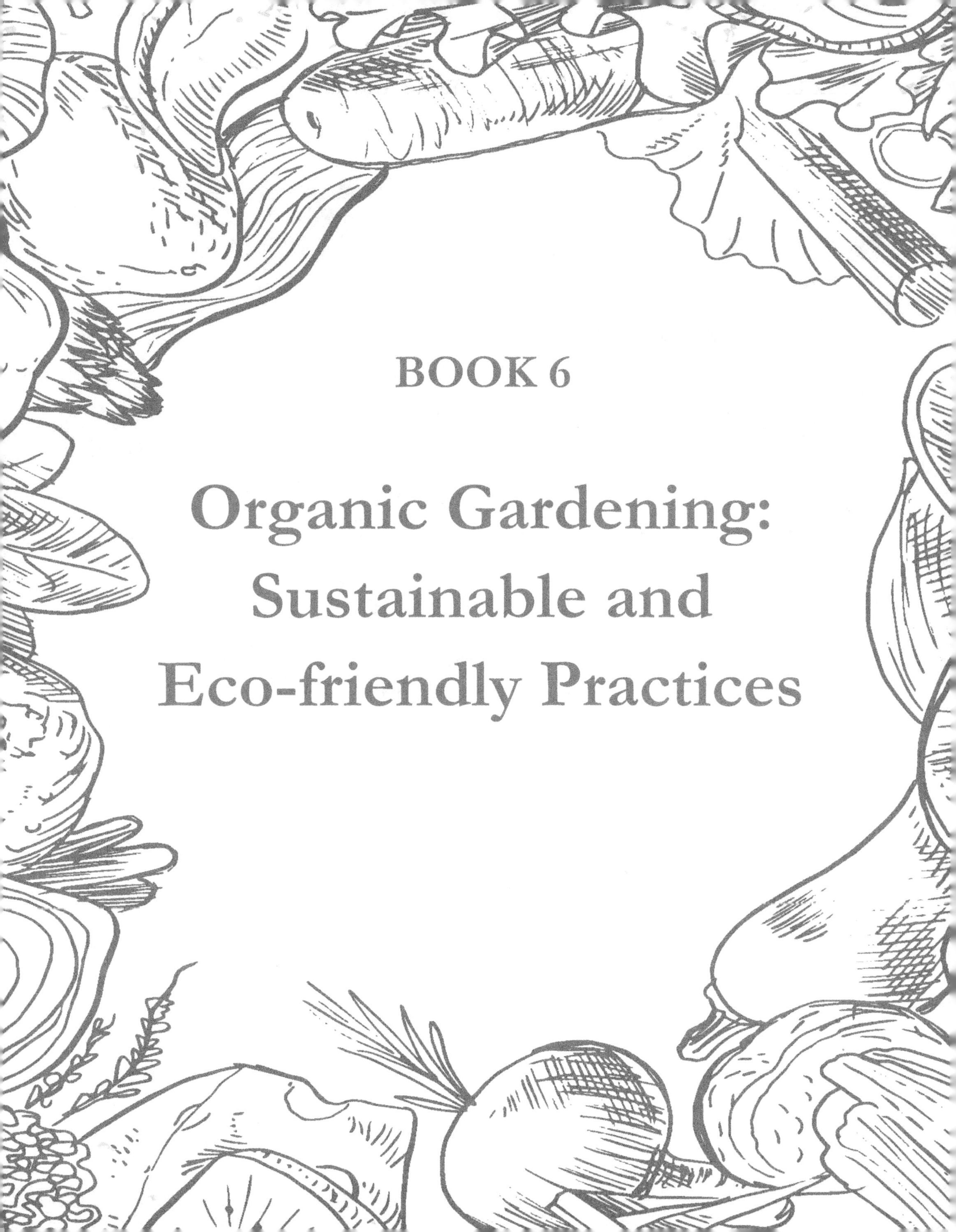

BOOK 6

Organic Gardening: Sustainable and Eco-friendly Practices

Book 6: Organic Gardening: Sustainable and Eco-friendly Practices

Introduction

In recent years people have come to realize the impact of conventional farming practices and the importance of transitioning, to sustainable methods. Organic gardening has emerged as a solution that not only benefits the environment but also promotes the production of nutritious food and other natural resources. Additionally organic gardening has gained popularity as it represents a mindset focused on preserving our planet and its inhabitants through comprehensive efforts.

Unlike conventional gardening, which heavily relies on fertilizers, pesticides and genetically modified organisms organic gardening emphasizes harnessing natural processes to cultivate healthy plants and soil. This distinction is significant since conventional gardening heavily relies on artificial inputs

In farming soil quality holds importance; hence maintaining its health is paramount. Organic farmers and gardeners place a premium, on building and sustaining soil because they understand that it forms the foundation for agriculture.

Instead of relying on fertilizers organic gardeners opt for compost cover crops and other natural additives to replenish the soils nutrients and beneficial microbes. This approach enhances the soil's structure enabling it to retain water and increasing availability. As a result plants grow stronger while minimizing soil erosion.

Compared to gardening practices that often involve pesticide use, water contamination and harm to insects, in the garden, organic gardening promotes biodiversity and ecological balance. To attract insects that act as natural pest controllers organic gardeners encourage plant growth and utilize companion planting techniques. When the ecosystem is restored to health there is no reliance on chemical pesticides as nature resumes its role, in regulating pest populations.

Weed control is an aspect of farming instead of resorting to chemical pesticides gardeners rely on manual weeding and mulching techniques to suppress weed growth. This not only prevents substances from entering the ecosystem but also improves soil health and fertility as organic matter decomposes.

In gardening practices great value is placed on using pollinated and heritage seed varieties.
Gardeners can avoid reliance on industrial seed suppliers. This approach helps protect regional plant varieties making them more resilient to changes and better suited for their specific areas.

The advantage is further enhanced by farming's emphasis on water usage. Proper implementation of drip irrigation, rainwater collection and mulching can conserve water reduce waste and maximize water efficiency.

The benefits of organic gardening go beyond gardens as it improves both the environment and the health of those who consume its products. Organic food is grown without chemicals, ensuring it doesn't contain any toxic residues. Following these standards makes produce safer, for consumption. Additionally preserving biodiversity and maintaining soils contribute to carbon storage. Help mitigate climate change.

The Principles and Benefits of Organic Gardening

One of the core principles in gardening is to avoid the use of chemicals. This means refraining from using pesticides, herbicides and synthetic fertilizers. Organic farmers consider this practice as an aspect of their approach. Instead they rely on strategies that effectively combat pests without causing harm.

The emphasis on balance is another principle in organic gardening. By cultivating a range of plants and employing companion planting techniques organic gardeners attract insects and pollinators to their gardens. These insects play a role in pest control and contribute to the overall enhancement of the gardens ecosystem.

In addition organic gardening places importance on maintaining soil for long lasting and productive horticulture. Organic gardeners prioritize the use of matter compost, cover crops and other natural amendments to build and nurture soil. These practices improve soil structure, water retention capacity and nutrient availability – all factors for plant growth.

Preserving seeds holds value in farming as it encourages the use of heirloom and open pollinated seed varieties whenever possible.
Gardeners play a role in preserving heirloom. Locally adapted plant varieties by saving and exchanging seeds. This practice helps maintain diversity and strengthen plant populations ensuring their survival.

One of the benefits of gardening is its eco friendly approach to water usage. By implementing practices like drip irrigation, rainwater collection and mulching gardeners promote water conservation. These methods maximize the use of this resource while minimizing wastage.

Organic gardening offers advantages. Firstly it is safer for the environment compared to conventional gardening because it avoids the use of harmful chemicals. By refraining from pesticides and fertilizers organic gardeners reduce harm and contribute to the preservation of ecosystems and their inhabitants.

Furthermore gardening emphasis on soil care and improvement leads to soil structure increased nutrient accessibility and enhanced microbial activity. Healthy soil plays a role in mitigating climate change through its impact on plant growth, erosion rates and carbon dioxide absorption.

Foods that are rich in nutrients, without any additives, are often referred to as "dense" or "chemical free" foods. When it comes to food, there are no chemicals involved in its production. Unlike fruits, vegetables and herbs that are grown with the use of chemical fertilizers and pesticides the ones cultivated through methods not taste better and offer more nutritional value but also ensure a safer consumption experience, for humans.

One of the benefits of gardening practices is that they contribute to biodiversity conservation. By creating an environment that supports a range of plants and beneficial insects organic gardens foster ecosystems. These ecosystems have resilience against diseases and insect infestations while also playing a role in sustaining pollinators vital for global food supply.

Another advantage of organic farming is the reduced reliance on chemical pesticides and fertilizers. This significantly lowers health risks associated with consuming produce benefiting gardeners, farmers and consumers. Ultimately embracing gardening practices leads to an agriculture system that's more environmentally friendly due to its focus, on maintaining and enhancing soil health.

To ensure the long term sustainability of farming systems for generations it is crucial to prioritize natural processes and minimize reliance, on external inputs. This approach not only benefits food security but also contributes to environmental preservation and stability

Implementing Organic Soil Management and Fertilization Techniques (G)

Organic gardening emphasizes sustainable methods that place a priority on soil health and fertility, and organic soil management and fertilization techniques are essential elements of this approach. Organic gardeners can grow healthy plants, enhance ecosystem health, and generate nutrient-rich, chemical-free food by nourishing the soil using natural ways." (the word 'may' might imply permission rather than ability)

1. Organic Soil Amendments:

a) **Compost**: The cornerstone of organic soil management is compost. It is produced by the breakdown of organic materials, including plant debris, yard trash, and kitchen leftovers, into nutrient-rich humus. Aeration, water retention, and soil structure are all improved by compost, which promotes a wholesome and fruitful growth environment. Compost also encourages the growth of helpful microbes, which aid in the cycling of nutrients and the prevention of illness.

b) **Cover Crops**: Also referred to as green manure, cover crops are sown to protect and enhance the soil while the primary crops are dormant. As they are integrated back into the soil, they aid in preventing erosion, control weed growth, and contribute organic matter. The need for extra fertilizers is decreased by the ability of cover crops, especially legumes like vetch and clover, to fix nitrogen from the air and make it accessible to succeeding crops.

c) **Mulching**: Mulching is a procedure in which organic materials like straw, leaves, or wood chips are spread over the soil's surface. Mulches aid in controlling soil temperature, weed development, and moisture retention. By adding organic matter to the soil as the mulch decomposes, the soil becomes more fertile.

2. Vermicomposting:

This specialized kind of composting uses earthworms to break down organic waste. The organic debris is broken down by earthworms, who then produce nutrient-rich worm castings that significantly increase soil fertility. Vermicompost is an excellent complement to organic agriculture since it improves soil structure and offers crucial nutrients.

3. Crop Rotation:

A tried-and-true organic approach, crop rotation is progressively switching the kinds of crops cultivated in a certain region from season to season. Different plant families need different amounts of nutrients and are more vulnerable to certain pests and diseases. Organic gardeners avoid nutrient depletion, lessen the development of pests and diseases, and preserve a healthy soil ecology by rotating their crops.

4. Nutrient Management:

To emulate natural processes, organic gardeners concentrate on slowly releasing nutrients to plants. Instead of using synthetic fertilizers, they depend on natural mineral supplements and organic sources of nutrients like compost. Organic fertilizers release nutrients gradually, limiting the runoff of nutrients and the leaching of surplus nutrients into the environment.

5. **Soil Testing and pH Management**:
For organic gardeners to precisely understand the nutrient levels and pH of the soil, soil testing is crucial. With the help of the findings of a soil test, gardeners may decide what nutrients their crops specifically require and, if necessary, modify the pH of the soil. To get the pH into the ideal range for the plants being cultivated, organic additions like sulfur or lime might be added.

6. **No-till and Reduced Tillage:**
Plowing or other forms of tillage may alter the soil's structure and cause erosion. To maintain soil health, organic gardeners often use no-till or low tillage techniques. These techniques support overall soil health and fertility by preserving soil structure, boosting organic matter retention, and lowering soil erosion.

Discovering Organic Soil Amendments:

1. **Compost**:
Gardeners may either make their own compost on-site or buy it from vendors. Compost is an essential organic soil component. Compost is created by a process known as composting, in which microbes and helpful insects break down organic waste products including kitchen scraps, yard debris, leaves, straw, and plant leftovers. This produces nutrient-rich humus that enhances the structure and fertility of the soil. Essential macro- and micronutrients like nitrogen, phosphorus, potassium, and trace minerals are provided by compost, fostering the development of healthy plants. Compost also improves soil texture, encourages beneficial microbial activity, and increases soil water-holding capacity and drainage. Compost may be placed on the garden beds or incorporated into the soil prior to planting to be used efficiently. Compost is a crucial element of organic gardening because it helps restore and maintain soil richness.

2. **Cover Crops**:
Also referred to as "green manure," cover crops are a particular plant species that are planted to cover and safeguard the soil while the primary crops are dormant. These cover crops perform a number of crucial tasks for bettering the soil. For instance:

- **Nitrogen Fixation**: Leguminous cover crops like clover, vetch, and peas have the ability to fix nitrogen from the atmosphere into the soil through a symbiotic relationship with nitrogen-fixing bacteria. This process enriches the soil with nitrogen, a crucial nutrient for plant growth.
- **Organic Matter Addition**: When cover crops are cut or tilled back into the soil, they add organic matter, which improves soil structure, enhances microbial activity, and increases nutrient availability.
- **Erosion Prevention**: Cover crops help protect the soil from erosion by stabilizing it with their root systems.
- **Weed Suppression**: Cover crops can suppress weed growth, reducing competition for nutrients and water.

Based on particular soil development objectives and the requirements of succeeding crops, cover crops might be selected. They provide several advantages for soil health and fertility and are often planted during fallow seasons or in between major crop rotations.

3. **Natural Mineral Supplements**:

In certain instances, nutritional deficits or imbalances that organic matter alone cannot correct may be discovered by soil testing. To add particular nutrients to the soil, utilize natural mineral supplements. Common illustrations include:

- **Rock Dust**: Rock dust contains a broad spectrum of trace minerals, such as calcium, magnesium, iron, and zinc, which can be lacking in some soils. These minerals are essential for plant growth and contribute to overall soil health.
- **Lime**: Lime is used to raise soil pH if it is too acidic. It also provides calcium and magnesium, which are important nutrients for plants.
- **Sulfur**: Sulfur is used to lower soil pH if it is too alkaline.
- **Bone Meal**: Bone meal is a natural source of phosphorus, a vital nutrient for root development and flower/fruit formation.
- **Kelp Meal**: Kelp meal is a source of potassium, essential for plant health and overall vigor.

In order to prevent overapplication and preserve the soil's nutritional balance, it is essential to apply these supplements sparingly and in accordance with the findings of soil testing.

Importance of Soil Testing and Creating a Nutrient-Balanced Soil Environment:

Understanding the particular nutrient levels and pH of the soil via soil testing is essential for organic agriculture. The present nutrient content, cation exchange capacity (CEC), pH, and organic matter levels in the soil may all be learned by a thorough soil test.

When organic gardeners get the results of a soil test, they can:

1. **Address Nutrient Deficiencies**: Soil testing may assist detect any nutrient shortages, allowing gardeners to focus organic additions on the specific elements they need to provide. This guarantees that plants can get the nutrients they need for healthy development.
2. **Avoid Excessive Fertilization**: Even with organic fertilizers, excessive fertilizing may result in nutritional imbalances and other environmental problems. Gardeners can apply amendments more precisely thanks to soil testing, reducing waste and possible environmental impact.
3. **Adjust Soil pH**: Plant nutrient availability is greatly influenced by the pH of the soil. Gardeners may apply organic amendments like lime or sulfur to change the pH of the soil to the required range for the particular crops being produced after conducting soil testing to determine if it is acidic, neutral, or alkaline.
4. **Maintain Nutrient Balance**: By being aware of the amount of nutrients in their soil, organic gardeners may work to create a nutrient-balanced environment where the necessary nutrients are available in the proper ratios for robust plant development.
5. **Make Informed Crop Choices**: Soil testing provides gardeners with information on the compatibility of the soil for various crops. Gardeners may choose crops that are best suited to the soil conditions by taking into account the nutrient profile and pH of the soil.

It takes careful use of compost, cover crops, and natural mineral supplements, combined with appropriate crop rotation and timing of additions, to create a nutrient-balanced soil environment. Organic gardeners may maximize soil fertility and structure for the best plant development while reducing environmental effect by taking into account the demands of the plants, the unique properties of the soil, and the findings of soil testing.

Natural Methods for Pest and Disease Control (O)

Organic gardening aims to establish an equilibrium between harmful organisms like pests and diseases by adopting eco-friendly and non-intrusive practices. By avoiding the use of pesticides and other chemicals organic gardeners effectively manage pests and diseases without posing risks to the environment, humans or animals.

Friendly pest control methods;

a. **Control**; This involves employing organisms such as predators and parasites to combat pest populations. For example introducing ladybugs to control aphids using wasps for caterpillar management or utilizing predatory nematodes to reduce soil dwelling pests. By promoting the presence of insects organic gardeners can establish a natural balance that reduces harmful insect pest populations.

b) **Companion planting**; This refers to interplanting crops to promote their individual growth or deter pests naturally. Some plants release insecticides. Attract beneficial insects for the benefit of nearby crops. For instance, growing marigolds or basil near tomatoes not only enhances tomato flavor but also deters certain pests. Also deters certain pests. Planting marigolds or basil in proximity acts as a deterrent, against nematodes. There are types of barriers that can be used to prevent pests from reaching plants. For example covering rows with netting or using insect mesh can physically inhibit pests. Protect the plants from being eaten or having eggs laid on them. Another method is to use floating row covers, which not provide early season protection, from pests but also extend the growing season.

Crop Rotation

To control and prevent garden pests it's beneficial to practice crop rotation. This involves planting crops in areas of the garden each year. Crop rotation helps break disease cycles and prevents pathogens in the soil from spreading reducing the risk of soil transmitted diseases and maintaining soil health.

Sanitation Practices

Maintaining sanitation practices is vital for preventing disease spread. Properly disposing of plant debris, dead leaves and diseased plants can prevent the transmission and reinfection of diseases. Regular cleaning of gardening equipment also plays a role in preventing plant disease spread.

Disease-resistant Varieties

Another strategy for preventing or controlling garden diseases is to plant disease-resistant varieties.

Healthy Garden with Reduced Chemical Usage

By implementing these methods we can effectively control pests. Maintain a healthy garden without relying heavily on chemical solutions. Choosing plant varieties that're resistant to diseases allows for the reduction of chemical usage.

The Role of Soil Health

The health of the soil plays a role in enhancing both plant growth and disease resistance. Organic practices like composting and planting cover crops contribute to soil health, which in turn helps keep plants from diseases. To avoid creating conditions for illnesses it is important to practice irrigation techniques, such as watering the soil at the base of plants early in the morning and allowing leaves to dry out during the day. Organic gardeners can utilize sprays containing ingredients, like neem oil, garlic or copper to combat fungal and bacterial diseases by eliminating microorganisms. While natural alternatives may not provide eradication of pests or diseases they are often safer and more environmentally friendly compared to chemicals. These approaches prioritize maintaining ecosystem health and preserving balance.

Effective Pest and Disease Management

When organic gardeners employ a range of techniques and adapt their methods to suit the needs of their gardens they can effectively handle pests and diseases while promoting a thriving ecosystem.

Integrated Pest Management (IPM)

To control pest populations Integrated Pest Management (IPM) combines natural pest control methods into a program. This approach is both thorough and well organized. The main goal of IPM is to prioritize the use of treatments that are least harmful while also minimizing pest damage and protecting species and the natural environment from unnecessary disruption.

IPM Encompasses Actions

a. **Regularly monitoring** the gardens health enables gardeners to identify pests and diseases including their developmental stages. By observing any behavior or signs of infestation gardeners can address the issue before it escalates.

b. **Thresholds**; IPM helps determine when intervention is necessary based on predetermined levels of pest or disease presence. Gardeners utilize these guidelines to assess the severity of infestations and decide on the course of action.

c. **Cultural Control**; Crop rotation, companion planting and carefully timing when to plant crops are all examples of practices that play a role, in Integrated Pest Management (IPM). These methods create environments that're unfavorable for pests and diseases effectively disrupting their life cycles.

Biological Control and Mechanical Management

Biological control is a strategy used to reduce pest populations by introducing species or promoting their existence. In IPM, predators and parasitoids among enemies are encouraged to naturally control pest populations. Mechanical management methods involve removing pests from plants or setting up barriers to prevent infestations. This can include picking off pests setting traps or constructing barriers.

Chemical Control

In cases where non chemical pest management methods have proven ineffective Integrated Pest Management may consider using approved pesticides. However these pesticides are chosen with caution to minimize harm to organisms and the environment as a whole by prioritizing toxicity and targeted application.

Role of Soil Health and Learning from Observations

In gardens controlling pests and diseases heavily relies on maintaining the health and vitality of plants. This brings us to our point in understanding Integrated Pest Management principles .Plants that are strong and in health have a chance of surviving attacks, from pests and diseases. To promote plant growth it is important for gardeners to focus on maintaining high quality soil by adding amendments providing nutrients ensuring sufficient water supply and giving plants suitable sunlight.

Another important skill for gardeners is the ability to learn from observations. Being able to identify pests, diseases and beneficial species plays a role in making informed decisions about the most effective management strategies. It is essential for gardeners to be flexible and willing to adjust their approaches based on what works for their gardens.

Fostering Biodiversity

By fostering biodiversity in your garden you can help prevent the establishment of species such as pests and diseases. This brings us to another point on our list Maintaining balance growing a range of plant species and creating habitats, for beneficial insects all contribute to organic gardeners ability to naturally keep pests and diseases under control.

Composting and Recycling Practices to Maintain Soil Health.

Maintaining soil fertility, in gardening is crucial. One effective way to achieve this is through the use of nutrient rich soil amendments. Composting offers an sustainable approach to accomplish this goal. It involves converting resources like leftover food, yard clippings and garden debris into compost. Composting not only diverts them from landfills but also transforms them into a valuable resource that enriches the soil and fosters healthy plant growth

Composting Process

Composting essentially entails utilizing decomposition to convert waste such as food scraps, yard waste and garden remnants into compost that is abundant in humus. This process relies on microorganisms, bacteria, fungi and other species that aid in breaking down the matter.

To create compost effectively follow these basic steps:

1) Select a suitable location for your compost bin or designate an area in your garden for composting. You can purchase a made compost bin or create one at home using materials like wood, plastic or wire mesh It's important to place the compost container, on soil so that organisms living in the soil can easily access the composting materials.
2) Achieving the balance of "carbon rich materials, such, as dry leaves, straw and newspaper with "green" nitrogen rich materials like food scraps and fresh green plant debris is crucial for successful composting. For best results, aim for a C:N ratio of 25 to 30, where C represents carbon and N represents nitrogen.

3) Aerating the compost pile by turning it helps hasten decomposition by providing oxygen to the microbes. Its recommended to turn the compost frequently using a pitchfork or other suitable tools.

4) For decomposition ensure that your compost pile measures least three feet wide and three feet tall. Smaller stacks may not generate heat to effectively break down the materials.

5) Keep in mind that composting is a process that requires patience. The time it takes for composting to complete can vary depending on factors like ingredients and conditions; it could range from a weeks to months before being ready, for use.

Benefits of Compost

Composting is a method, for improving soil quality. When compost is added to soil it brings about effects.

1) **Enhancing Soil Structure**; Firstly it enhances the structure of the soil by promoting particle aggregation resulting in improved porosity that allows water and air permeability. Additionally it helps reduce soil compaction, which in turn promotes root growth and enhances absorption by plants.

2) **Supplying Nutrients**; Compost serves as a source of both macro and micronutrients such as nitrogen, phosphorus, potassium, calcium and magnesium. These nutrients are gradually released over time ensuring a supply for plants.

3) **Retaining Water**; Moreover compost acts like a sponge that retains water within the soil. This helps maintain moisture levels during dry seasons when water may be scarce. As a result watering frequency can be reduced while still benefiting plant growth.

4) **Supporting Microbial Activity**; Furthermore compost contains microorganisms that contribute to soil health and increase microbial activity. These microorganisms play a role in preventing plant diseases by breaking down waste and releasing essential nutrients.

5) **pH Buffer**; Lastly compost has a pH buffer that helps maintain the optimal pH level of the soil. This makes it suitable for a wide range of plant species to thrive.

Sustainable Gardening with Composting

By utilizing composting techniques to amend soil quality in these ways mentioned above, gardeners can ensure plants have strong growth potential. Composting is a way for gardeners to cut down on using chemical fertilizers making it an appealing choice, for sustainable gardening. This helps minimize the risk of fertilizer runoff into water sources and lessens its impact on the environment. By incorporating compost into the soil gardeners can gradually enhance soil health and fertility by boosting its matter content over time.

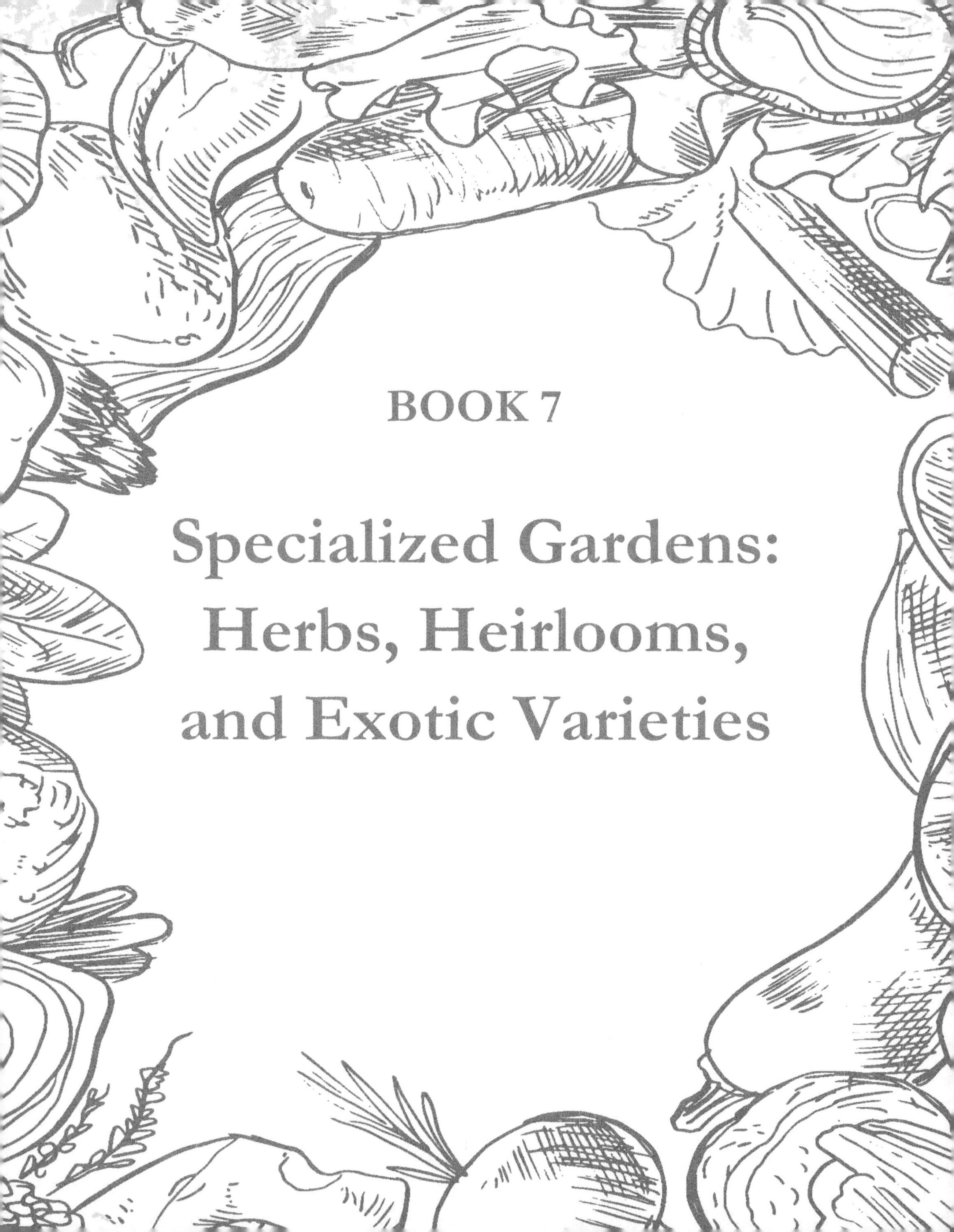

BOOK 7

Specialized Gardens: Herbs, Heirlooms, and Exotic Varieties

Book 7: Specialized Gardens: Herbs, Heirlooms, and Exotic Varieties

Introduction

Creating gardens dedicated to herbs, heirlooms and exotic plant species can be a fulfilling way to broaden your gardening interests. These unique gardens focus on groups of plants showcasing their qualities, fascinating histories and diverse cultural origins. Now let's delve deeper into each of these garden types;

1) **Herb Gardens**; Herb gardens are designed to cultivate a variety of herbs that can be used for cooking, medicinal purposes and aromatherapy. Throughout generations people have come to appreciate the benefits, culinary versatility and captivating fragrances offered by these plants. In an herb garden, you can grow herbs like mint, thyme, rosemary and oregano as well as more unusual varieties like lemon balm, tarragon or stevia. A maintained herb garden serves purposes such as providing fresh ingredients, for cooking delightful dishes or creating herbal remedies, immersing you in a pleasant sensory experience.

2) **Heirloom Plants**; Heirloom plants are those that have been passed down from one generation to another through open pollination methods. This preservation technique ensures that these plant varieties retain their characteristics over time.

To minimize the loss of biodiversity heirloom gardens have a role, in cultivating and preserving traditional plant varieties. They help prevent the disappearance of farming practices and regional cuisines that have been affected by the use of hybridized crops. One effective approach is to focus on growing food and floral heirlooms.

3) **Exotic Varieties Gardens**; Another type of garden known as Exotic Varieties Garden or Varieties Garden aims to safeguard unusual and non native plant species from around the world. By showcasing plant species that are not commonly found in the environment these gardens educate visitors about the flora and fauna existing in different regions worldwide. Exotic gardens often feature subtropical plants known for their uniqueness and beauty. Exploring these gardens allows visitors to deepen their understanding of botany and horticulture while developing an appreciation for the wonders of the plant world.

Benefits of Specialized Gardens

- **Education**; Visitors can learn extensively about the origins, care and practical applications of plant species.
- **Conservation**; The preservation of rare and endangered plant species is an objective for both heirloom gardeners as well as those managing exotic gardens
- **Delightful Culinary Experiences**. Growing herb gardens offer an abundance of flavorful herbs for kitchen use
- **Therapeutic Benefits**; Therapeutic gardens often cultivate herbs that have been scientifically proven to have impacts on mental well-being.
- **Exquisite Displays**; Exquisite gardens are visually captivating, showcasing plants arranged in eye-catching displays

Challenges of Specialized Gardens

- **Climate Requirements**; Certain exotic and heirloom plants come with climate requirements, making them more challenging to cultivate in some regions
- **Expertise and Maintenance**; Specialized gardens that house these unique plants may require a certain level of gardening expertise and higher maintenance.
- **Accessibility**; Locating heirloom and exotic plant varieties can be a bit challenging since they might not be readily available at nurseries

Growing and Caring for a Diverse Range of Herbs for Culinary and Medicinal Purposes

An experience that is pleasant and enlightening is one in which one cultivates and tends to a wide variety of herbs for use in both culinary and medicinal preparations. Herbs have been used for culinary enrichment and natural treatments for many years They provide a diverse range of tastes, aromas, and medicinal effects. Let's examine how to grow and care for common culinary herbs such as basil, parsley, and rosemary, as well as how to cultivate herbs for their therapeutic properties:

1. Cultivating Culinary Herbs:

a) Basil

1. **Growing**: Basil thrives in warm, sunny locations with well-draining soil. Start by sowing seeds indoors and transplanting the seedlings outdoors after the last frost date. Alternatively, you can purchase young basil plants from a nursery. Pinch off the flowers to encourage leaf growth.
2. **Care**: Water basil regularly but avoid overwatering. Harvest the leaves regularly to promote continuous growth, and pinch off any flower buds to prevent the plant from going to seed.

b) Parsley

1. Growing: Parsley can be grown from seeds or transplanted seedlings. It prefers rich, moist soil and partial shade, especially in hot climates. Soak parsley seeds in warm water for a day before planting to improve germination rates.
2. Care: Keep the soil consistently moist, and mulch around the plants to retain moisture. Regularly harvest outer leaves to encourage new growth and prevent the plant from bolting.

c) Rosemary

1. Growing: Rosemary enjoys full sun and well-draining soil. It's best propagated from cuttings or purchased as young plants. In colder regions, it can be grown in containers and brought indoors during winter.
2. Care: Rosemary is relatively drought-tolerant once established. Water it deeply but infrequently. Prune lightly to maintain its shape and size, and harvest sprigs as needed.

d) Mint

1. Growing: Mint prefers rich, moist soil and partial shade, although it can tolerate some sun. It's best grown from young plants or cuttings, as it can spread aggressively if grown from seeds.
2. Care: Keep the soil consistently moist, as mint has a high water requirement. To control its growth, consider growing it in containers. Pinch back the tips regularly to encourage bushier growth.

e) Thyme

1. Growing: Thyme thrives in well-draining, sandy soil and full sun. It can be propagated from cuttings or purchased as young plants. Space the plants adequately to allow for air circulation.
2. Care: Water thyme moderately, allowing the soil to dry out between waterings. Prune lightly after flowering to maintain shape and encourage new growth.

f) Cilantro (Coriander)

1. Growing: Cilantro prefers cool temperatures and partial sun. It can be grown from seeds directly in the garden, as it doesn't transplant well. Successive plantings every few weeks ensure a continuous harvest.
2. Care: Keep the soil consistently moist, especially during hot weather. Harvest the leaves for culinary use and the seeds (coriander) before the plant bolts and goes to seed

2. Cultivating Medicinal Herbs

a) Chamomile

1. Growing: Chamomile prefers well-draining, sandy soil and partial sun. It can be grown from seeds or nursery-bought seedlings. Thin the seedlings to allow proper spacing.
2. Care: Keep the soil evenly moist but not waterlogged. Harvest the flowers when they are fully open, and dry them for use in teas and other remedies.

b) Lavender

1. Growing: Lavender thrives in well-draining soil and full sunlight. Propagate it from cuttings or purchase young plants. Space them apart to improve air circulation and reduce disease risk.
2. Care: Lavender is drought-tolerant once established. Water sparingly and avoid wetting the foliage. Prune after flowering to maintain shape and encourage new growth.

c) Echinacea (Purple Coneflower)

1. Growing: Echinacea prefers fertile, well-draining soil and full sun. It can be grown from seeds or purchased as young plants. Sow the seeds in the fall for better germination rates.
2. Care: Water regularly during its first growing season. Once established, it becomes relatively drought-tolerant. Harvest the roots and flower heads for medicinal use.

d) Peppermint

1. Growing: Peppermint requires rich, moist soil and partial shade, although it can tolerate some sun. It's best propagated from root divisions or young plants.
2. Care: Water peppermint regularly to keep the soil moist. Mulch around the plants to retain moisture and suppress weeds. Harvest the leaves for medicinal purposes as needed.

e) Lemon Balm

1. Growing: Lemon balm prefers well-draining soil and partial shade. It can be grown from seeds or young plants. Space the plants adequately to allow for their spreading growth habit.

2. Care: Water lemon balm regularly to keep the soil evenly moist. Prune the plant after flowering to prevent it from becoming leggy. Harvest the leaves for herbal teas and other remedies.

f) Sage

1. Growing: Sage prefers well-draining soil and full sun. It's best propagated from cuttings or young plants. Space the plants to allow for good air circulation.
2. Care: Sage is relatively drought-tolerant once established. Water it moderately, and avoid overwatering. Prune the plant regularly to promote bushier growth and prevent legginess.

General Tips for Herb Cultivation:

- Most herbs prefer well-draining soil to avoid root rot.
- Regular pruning and harvesting promote bushier growth and prevent plants from becoming woody.
- Mulching around herbs helps retain moisture and suppresses weeds.
- Many herbs benefit from being grown in containers, especially if you have limited space or poor soil.

To successfully cultivate herbs, it is vital to understand their individual requirements and growing conditions, just like any other kind of gardening project. Be sure to do your homework and have a good understanding of the needs of the herbs you want to cultivate in order to reap the culinary and medicinal benefits they provide. Enjoy exploring the world of herbs and learning about the various ways in which they can enhance your culinary experiences and contribute to your overall health.

General Tips for Culinary and Medicinal Herbs:

- Most herb benefit from a balanced fertilizer application during the growing season.
- Regularly inspect the plants for signs of pests or diseases, taking appropriate measures if needed.
- Be mindful during harvesting, ensuring that you leave enough foliage for the plant to continue growing.

Exploring Heirloom Vegetables and Their Historical Significance

Not only is investigating heirloom vegetables and learning about their rich history an adventure into the past, but it is also a way to ensure that future generations will have access to a genetically diverse and culturally significant food supply. Vegetables are considered heirloom if they are of an open-pollinated variety and have been in the same family or community for at least fifty years, and frequently for a considerably longer period of time. These seeds are kept and passed down from one growing season to the next, helping to ensure that their distinctive qualities and aromas are preserved. In this lesson, we will discuss the significance of heritage vegetables, as well as look at many noteworthy kinds and how to raise them:

Importance of Heirloom Vegetables:

1. **Genetic Diversity**: Heirloom vegetables are an essential component in the maintenance of a diverse genetic pool among plant species. The use of hybrid varieties in modern agriculture has become more common as a result of selective breeding for certain characteristics such as uniformity and shelf life. Nevertheless, because of this, there has been a decline in the gene pool, which has made crops more susceptible to diseases, pests, and changing environmental circumstances. Through their unique genetic makeup, heirloom varieties contribute to the preservation of a pool of potentially useful characteristics that may be used in subsequent breeding and adaptation efforts.

2. **Cultural Heritage**: Heirloom vegetables are more than just plants; rather, they are living representations of a culture's history and tradition. These seeds, which have been handed down from one generation to the next, are the keepers of a long line of traditions, tales, and culinary customs. They often have strong links to their local culture and location, and their flavor profiles frequently mirror those of the communities that have fostered them over the course of generations.

3. **Unique Flavors**: Heirloom veggies are highly regarded for their excellent tastes, which may be noticeably distinct from those of their contemporary analogues. Because the seeds have not been subjected to significant breeding for the sake of mass production, they have been able to keep their authentic flavor, fragrance, and consistency. As a result, they are a gold mine for cooks and foodies who are looking for genuine and unique dining experiences to partake in.

Heirloom Vegetable Varieties and Growing Tips:

1. **Brandywine Tomato**:
    - Characteristics: One of the most famous heirloom tomatoes, Brandywine, boasts large, pinkish-red fruits with a rich, sweet flavor and low acidity.
    - Growing: Start the seeds indoors 6-8 weeks before the last frost date. Transplant the seedlings outside after the danger of frost has passed. Provide support as the plants can grow quite tall. Regularly prune the suckers for better fruit production.

2. **Moon and Stars Watermelon**:
    - Characteristics: This unique heirloom watermelon features dark green skin speckled with yellow spots, resembling a night sky with stars. The flesh is sweet and juicy, with black seeds.
    - Growing: Sow the seeds directly into well-prepared soil after the last frost date. Provide plenty of space for the vines to spread. Watermelons require warm temperatures and regular watering.

3. **Scarlet Runner Bean**:
    - Characteristics: Scarlet Runner Bean is not only a great edible but also an ornamental plant with beautiful red flowers. The beans are tender, flavorful, and a favorite in soups and stews.
    - Growing: Soak the seeds overnight before planting to enhance germination. Provide support for the climbing vines. Harvest the beans when they are young and tender.

4. **Golden Bantam Sweet Corn**:
    - Characteristics: This sweet corn variety produces small, golden-yellow kernels bursting with sweetness and flavor.
    - Growing: Plant the seeds in blocks rather than rows for better pollination. Corn is wind-pollinated, so spacing is essential. Harvest the ears when the kernels are plump and milky.

5. **Early White Bush Scallop Squash**:
    - Characteristics: This heirloom summer squash has scalloped edges and a creamy white color. It has a delicate, nutty flavor.
    - Growing: Plant the seeds directly in the garden after the last frost date. Space the plants to allow for good air circulation. Harvest the squash when they are small and tender.

It is possible to cultivate heritage vegetable varieties in a manner that is similar to that of farming current varieties; nevertheless, it is essential to pay attention to the specific qualities and needs of each variety as it grows.

Here are some basic recommendations for cultivating heirloom vegetables:

- Choose open-pollinated seeds from reputable sources to ensure the authenticity of heirloom varieties.
- Consider saving seeds from your heirloom vegetables to continue the tradition and maintain their genetic integrity.
- Practice organic gardening methods to preserve the purity of heirloom varieties and promote healthier plants.
- Embrace imperfections in appearance as heirloom vegetables may not have the uniformity of modern hybrids, but they more than make up for it in flavor and history.

Introduction to Unique and Exotic Vegetable Varieties and Their Cultivation

Rare and unusual vegetable types provide an enticing and varied spectrum of tastes, colors, and textures, which may take one's culinary experiences to fascinating new levels. Your knowledge of the diversity of agricultural production throughout the world may be deepened and your exposure to a variety of ethnic cuisines broadened by the exploration of these lesser-known veggies. Growing rare and unusual veggies in your garden may introduce you to a whole new world of delicious experiences and opportunities.

The following is a list of some of the most interesting vegetables, along with information on how to produce them:

1. **Dragon Fruit (Pitaya)**:
    - **Characteristics**: Dragon fruit is a stunningly beautiful tropical fruit with vibrant pink or white flesh studded with black seeds. It has a mildly sweet, refreshing taste, reminiscent of a cross between a pear and a kiwi.
    - **Growing**: Dragon fruit grows best in warm climates with well-draining soil and full sunlight. It can also be grown in containers. Provide a sturdy trellis or support for the climbing cacti-like plants.

2. **Romanesco Broccoli**:
    - **Characteristics**: Romanesco broccoli, also known as Roman cauliflower, is an eye-catching vegetable with lime-green, spiraled florets forming fractal patterns. It has a delicate, nutty flavor.
    - **Growing**: Romanesco broccoli prefers cool climates and well-draining, fertile soil. It's similar to growing regular broccoli or cauliflower. Ensure adequate spacing to accommodate its unique head structure.

3. **Water Spinach (Kangkong)**:
    - **Characteristics**: Water spinach is a semi-aquatic plant with long, tender stems and leaves. It is widely used in Asian cuisines and has a slightly sweet and spinach-like flavor.
    - **Growing**: Water spinach grows well in moist soil or shallow water. It can be propagated from cuttings. Ensure it receives at least six hours of sunlight daily.

4. **Kohlrabi**:
    - **Characteristics**: Kohlrabi is a member of the brassica family and resembles a turnip with a stem-like bulb above the ground. It has a mild, slightly sweet taste with hints of cabbage and broccoli.
    - **Growing**: Kohlrabi thrives in cool climates and well-draining soil. Sow seeds directly in the garden and thin the seedlings to allow for proper bulb development.

5. **Jicama**:
    - **Characteristics**: Jicama, also known as the Mexican yam bean, is a root vegetable with a crisp, juicy texture and a sweet, nutty flavor.
    - **Growing**: Jicama prefers warm climates with well-draining soil. It requires a long growing season, and its vines need support as they climb.

6. **Oca**:
    - **Characteristics**: Oca, also known as New Zealand yam, is a tuberous vegetable with a tangy, lemony taste. It comes in various colors, from yellow and pink to red and purple.
    - **Growing**: Oca is a frost-sensitive plant that thrives in cool, moist climates. Plant the tubers in the spring, and harvest them in the fall after the foliage has died back.

Cultivating Unique and Exotic Vegetables:

- **Research**: Learn about the specific requirements of each vegetable variety, including soil preferences, temperature tolerance, and water needs. Understanding their growth habits is essential for successful cultivation.
- **Seed Selection**: Look for reputable seed suppliers that specialize in unique and exotic vegetable varieties. Ensure the seeds are fresh and of good quality to maximize germination rates.
- **Growing Conditions**: Provide the right growing conditions based on the vegetables' native environments. Some may require full sun, while others may thrive in partial shade. Tailor your garden accordingly.
- **Soil Preparation**: Prepare the soil by incorporating organic matter and ensuring good drainage. Adjust the soil pH if needed to suit the vegetables' preferences.
- **Watering**: Water the plants regularly, but avoid overwatering, as it can lead to root rot or other problems. Monitor the soil moisture and adjust watering accordingly.
- **Pest and Disease Management**: Keep an eye out for common pests and diseases that may affect these vegetables. Employ organic pest control methods whenever possible to maintain their unique flavors and characteristics.
- **Harvesting**: Follow proper harvesting guidelines for each vegetable to ensure peak flavor and quality. Some may be best when harvested young, while others may require more time to develop their full potential.

It may be a wonderful and satisfying experience to broaden your gastronomic horizons by investigating rare and unusual types of vegetables that are grown in different parts of the globe. On your plate, these veggies will provide a variety of tastes, textures, and colors to the meal, giving you the opportunity to try out various recipes and cuisines. It is imperative that you educate yourself on the precise growth needs and cultivation methods of these uncommon vegetables before attempting to effectively include them into your garden.

The following is an in-depth tutorial that will assist you in getting started:

1. **Research and Select Exotic Varieties**:
    - Begin by researching and identifying exotic vegetable varieties that pique your interest. Look for vegetables that are well-suited to your climate and growing conditions. Consider the space available in your garden and choose vegetables that fit within your gardening capacity.
2. **Understanding Growing Requirements**:
    - Each exotic vegetable has specific growing requirements that may differ from traditional garden vegetables. Some key factors to consider are:
        1. **Climate**: Check if the vegetable thrives in your local climate – some may prefer tropical, subtropical, temperate, or cool climates.

2. **Sunlight**: Determine the sunlight needs of each vegetable – full sun, partial shade, or shade.
3. **Soil**: Examine soil preferences, such as well-draining soil, sandy loam, or rich organic soil. Some exotic vegetables may have specific pH preferences.
4. **Watering**: Learn about the watering needs of each vegetable – some may require more water, while others prefer drier conditions.
5. **Temperature**: Be aware of temperature sensitivity – some vegetables may be frost-tolerant, while others may require protection from cold temperatures.

3. **Seed Selection and Sourcing**:
    - Once you have identified the exotic vegetables you wish to grow, find reputable seed suppliers or nurseries that offer these varieties. Ensure that the seeds are fresh and authentic to maximize germination rates and maintain the unique characteristics of the plants.
4. **Soil Preparation**:
    - Prepare the soil in advance to meet the specific needs of each vegetable. Add compost or organic matter to improve soil fertility and structure. Adjust the pH if necessary to create the ideal growing environment.
5. **Planting and Care**:
    - Follow the recommended planting guidelines for each vegetable, including the depth and spacing of seeds or seedlings. Pay attention to proper planting times based on your local climate and frost dates.
6. **Watering and Fertilization**:
    - Regularly water your exotic vegetables according to their specific requirements. Monitor soil moisture levels and adjust watering as needed. Be cautious not to overwater, as excessive moisture can lead to root rot or other issues.
    - Apply organic fertilizers based on the nutrient needs of each vegetable. Avoid excessive use of synthetic fertilizers, as they may alter the unique flavors and characteristics of the vegetables.
7. **Pest and Disease Management**:
    - Be vigilant for pests and diseases that may affect your exotic vegetables. Implement organic pest control methods such as companion planting, handpicking pests, and using natural repellents.
8. **Harvesting**:
    - Familiarize yourself with the optimal harvest times for each vegetable. Harvesting at the right stage ensures the best flavor and texture. Some exotic vegetables may have specific signs that indicate their readiness for harvest.
9. **Culinary Exploration**:
    - As your exotic vegetables mature, explore their culinary potential in a variety of dishes and cuisines. Experiment with traditional recipes from the regions where these vegetables originate or create new and exciting culinary combinations.
10. **Seed Saving:**
    - Consider saving seeds from your successfully grown exotic vegetables. Seed saving helps preserve the genetic diversity of these unique varieties and ensures their availability for future cultivation.

BOOK 8

Troubleshooting: Identifying and Solving Garden Problems

Book 8: Troubleshooting: Identifying and Solving Garden Problems

Introduction

Gardening is a truly fulfilling hobby that allows people to connect with the natural world, create beautiful outdoor spaces, and even grow their own food. However, like any endeavor, it comes with its challenges. Environmental factors, pesky pests, illnesses, and yes, even our own human errors can all take a toll on our beloved gardens. But fear not, for with a keen eye and a bit of know-how, we can keep our gardens healthy and thriving.

The Importance of Problem-Solving in Gardening

In this guide, we'll delve into the art of identifying and fixing garden problems. We'll explore the essential steps to maintain a tip-top garden, from recognizing issues to uncovering their root causes and implementing lasting solutions. Whether you're a seasoned green thumb or just starting out, the valuable information here will equip you with the tools you need to tackle a wide range of gardening challenges.

Early Detection and Precautions

As any skilled gardener knows, being able to solve problems as they arise is key. By being proactive and catching issues early on, we can prevent serious damage and financial woes. Simply observing your plants' growth patterns, leaf color, and overall health can reveal valuable clues. These subtle changes might be signs of underlying problems. Armed with this knowledge, gardeners can make informed decisions on how to address issues, avoiding the pitfalls of untested or harmful solutions.

Awareness of Garden Issues

Having a thorough awareness of the range of issues that may develop in a garden is crucial before beginning the process of problem-solving. Among the most frequent issues are:

a) **Insects and Pests;** They can wreak havoc on a plant's leaves, stems, and fruits if they get a hold of it
b) **Plant diseases**; fungi, bacteria, and viruses can quickly spread across a garden, causing death, discoloration, and deterioration.
c) **Nutrient Deficiencies**; Leaves will become yellow and the plant will not grow if it doesn't have enough nitrogen, phosphate, and potassium.
d) **Environmental Stress**; such as that caused by high temperatures, prolonged drought, or soggy soil, can compromise a plant's defenses, leaving it vulnerable to disease and pests.
e) **Soil Problems**; Root growth and nutrient uptake can be stunted by soil problems such poor structure, pH imbalance, and compaction.
f) **Weeds**: Unwanted plants can be a major annoyance if they are allowed to grow unchecked and compete with desired crops for food and water.

The Troubleshooting Methodology

Identifying and fixing garden issues requires a methodical approach to ensure effective solutions. Here is a detailed procedure to follow when troubleshooting garden problems:

- **Pay Special Attention to Plants;** Pay special attention to the growth and look of each plant in your garden by conducting regular inspections. Keep an eye out for anything out of the ordinary.
- **Conduct research**; Consult dependable gardening resources, such as books or internet forums, to determine what might be causing the problems. At this stage, you should know a lot about different types of plants and what they need to thrive.
- **Diagnosis;** Use what you've learned from your observations and your research to make an educated guess as to what's causing the symptoms.
- **Implement a Solution**; After the root of the problem has been isolated, the following stage is to implement a workable solution. Natural remedies, cultural practices, and even the judicious application of pharmacological therapy are all viable options in this regard.
- **Close Observation and Patience**; After the treatment has been applied, close observation of the affected plants is required to ascertain that the issue is indeed being resolved. You may need to make some changes to your strategy and be patient until the effects of your efforts take effect

Preventative Measures

Taking preventative measures is essential for the continued health of a garden, in addition to dealing with issues when they develop. Many gardening problems could be avoided with the use of preventative measures including crop rotation, sufficient irrigation, mulching, and meticulous hygiene.

You can save some effort and time by doing this.

A healthy garden requires a balance of nutrients, the absence of pests and illnesses, and the provision of adequate protection from the elements. However, this equilibrium may be disrupted by a number of events, leading to food shortages, diseases, and pest problems. A gardener's ability to correctly identify these issues is crucial for developing effective solutions.

Here, we'll go through some of the most frequently encountered garden problems, such as nutrient deficiencies, diseases, and pests, and how to identify them.

Identifying Vitamin and Mineral Deficiencies

Without the presence of nutrients, plant growth and development are impossible. When plants are lacking a necessary nutrient, they will show telltale signs that may help you identify the nutrient(s) they are deficient in.

Symptoms of common nutritional deficits include the following:

- Nitrogen (N) deficiency causes stunted growth, chlorosis (yellowing of older leaves), and diminished vitality in plants.
- Lack of phosphorus (P) causes plants to grow slowly, have dark green or purple leaves, and have underdeveloped root systems.
- A lack of potassium (K) can cause your plants to be more susceptible to disease and environmental challenges, as well as cause the edges of your leaves to burn.
- Interveinal chlorosis (yellowing) between the leaf veins is a symptom of iron insufficiency.
- A lack of magnesium (Mg) causes yellowing between the veins of the leaves, usually appearing first on the older leaves.
- Yellowing and abnormal leaf development are symptoms of zinc insufficiency.
- Young leaves may develop abnormally and the plant as a whole may be harmed by a lack of calcium (Ca).

To correct nutritional deficiencies, it may be necessary to use either well-balanced fertilizers or specialized nutrient supplements that are customized to the specific nutrient shortage that has been found. Soil testing can be useful for determining what kind of fertilizer is needed and what nutrient levels the soil currently has.

Identifying Frequent Garden Illnesses

If not stopped quickly, plant diseases can swiftly spread and severely harm crops.

Here are some indications of several common garden diseases:

- **Powdery Mildew**; White, powdery spots on the leaves, stems, and flowers are caused by Powdery Mildew, a fungal disease.
- **Downy Mildew**; Yellow patches on the upper leaf surface and a white, downy growth on the lower surface are indicative of Downy Mildew, another fungal disease.
- **Leaf Spot Diseases**; Diseases that produce leaf spots, leave tiny black spots on leaves, sometimes encircled by a yellow halo.
- **Rust Diseases**; Diseases caused by rust can be identified by the telltale rusty, orange, or brown spots that appear on leaves, stems, and flowers.
- **Blight**; Diseases that cause blight quickly turn plant tissues brown and kill them.

Careful observation of the diseased plants is required for an accurate diagnosis and the selection of a treatment plan. Look for distinct patterns or colors of lesions, as well as signs of fungal development or spores, in the affected area. To prevent the spread of disease, you should remove and dispose of infected plant parts and, if necessary, use fungicides designed for that purpose.

Garden Pest Identification

Damage can be done in a garden by insects, fungus, and other pests that feed on plants, spread illness, and prevent growth. Successful pest control relies on gardeners being able to recognize common garden pests and their telltale indications.

Some instances are as follows:

- **Aphids**; Aphids are little, soft-bodied insects that congregate on new growth, where they feed on plant juices and deform the leaves.
- **Caterpillars**; Caterpillars, on the other hand, eat leaves and usually leave behind holes in the leaves in addition to other harm.
- **Spider Mites**; Stippling and yellowing of leaves are caused by spider mites, small arachnids that feed on plant sap.
- **Whiteflies**: These tiny flying insects like to cluster on the undersides of leaves, where they feed on the sap and ultimately cause the leaves to turn yellow.
- **Slugs**; These slimy parasites eat irregular holes in foliage and fruits and leave behind trails of slime as they go.

To keep unwanted pests out of your garden, you may need to employ the usage of physical barriers, natural predators, or environmentally safe insecticides. Check on your plants frequently to catch pest problems early and prevent them from spreading.

Addressing Nutrient Deficiencies

a) **Organic Soil Amendments**:
Organic soil supplements, such as compost, well-rotted manure, and organic waste, are able to increase both the fertility of the soil and the nutrient content of the soil. These amendments not only offer a supply of nutrients that are released over a longer period of time, but they also improve the capacity of the soil to hold onto moisture and nutrients, which in turn promotes overall plant health.

b) **Balanced Fertilization Practices**:
Make use of balanced fertilizers, which are those that include a combination of both primary and secondary nutrients, such as calcium (Ca), magnesium (Mg), and sulfur (S). Primary nutrients include nitrogen (N), phosphorus (P), and potassium (K), while secondary nutrients include calcium (Ca), magnesium (Mg), and sulfur (S). It will be easier to avoid nutrient imbalances and shortages if you apply these fertilizers in accordance with the particular requirements of your plants and on the basis of the findings of a soil test.

c) **Foliar Feeding**:
If your plant is suffering from significant nutritional shortages or is going through a crucial development stage, foliar feeding may be an effective answer for you. Foliar sprays that contain water-soluble nutrients may be sprayed directly to the leaves of plants, enabling the plants to rapidly absorb the nutrients and more quickly recover from nutritional deficits.

d) **Mulching**:
The practice of covering garden beds with a layer of organic material, such as straw, wood chips, or leaves, helps to preserve the soil's moisture and warmth while also facilitating the cycling of nutrients. In addition to preventing the loss of nutrients via leaching and erosion, mulch makes for a healthier garden.

Organic and Integrated Pest Management (IPM) Strategies

- **Beneficial Insects**: Garden pests can be controlled by attracting beneficial insects like ladybugs, lacewings, and parasitic wasps. Ladybugs, lacewings, and parasitic wasps are all examples of such insects. You may attract many of these beneficial insects by planting flowers that provide them with nectar and pollen.
- **Crop Rotation**: Regularly rotating crops disrupts pest life cycles and reduces specific pest populations. Different plant families have varying vulnerabilities to attacks, making crop rotation an effective way to minimize pest invasions.
- **Companion Planting**: Interplanting diverse species that are compatible with each other can act as a natural insect repellent. Planting companion crops like marigolds and tomatoes can deter certain pests.
- **Physical Barriers**: To keep out larger insects and animals like birds and rabbits, put up physical barriers around your plants. Row coverings, netting, and collars are some types of physical barriers.
- **Neem Oil**: Neem Oil, a natural insecticide and fungicide, has the potential to be useful against numerous diseases and plant pests. To achieve this, it disrupts the pests' hormonal systems, rendering them unable to feed and multiply.
- **Insecticidal Soaps and Horticultural Oils**: These can be used to control soft-bodied insects including aphids, spider mites, and whiteflies. They work because the harmful insects are suffocated while the beneficial ones are spared.
- **Biological Controls**: Beneficial nematodes, bacteria, or fungi that prey on a particular pest or ailment are just a few examples of the biological controls that can be used to reduce its number.
- **Periodic Plant Inspections**: To catch pest infestations and disease outbreaks in their earliest stages, periodic plant inspections should be performed regularly. Taking preventative measures at the first sign of trouble is usually preferable.

The Value of Companion Planting and Crop Rotation in Sustainable Agriculture

Two important principles in sustainable and organic gardening are crop rotation and companion planting. These strategies enhance overall garden health and productivity while reducing reliance on artificial inputs and preserving biodiversity.

1. **Rotating Crops**: Planting different crops on the same field over several years protects against the buildup of specific pests and diseases and improves soil quality.

2. **Companion Planting**: Growing two or more different types of plants together can promote positive interactions. It can aid in pest control, enhance flavor, and maximize space and soil fertility.

By adopting these organic and integrated pest management strategies, gardeners can maintain a healthier and more balanced environment while effectively managing pests and promoting sustainable agriculture.

Crop Rotation Benefits

Some of crop rotation's most significant benefits include:

a) **Disease and Pest Control**: Many pests and diseases are host-specific, meaning they only infest certain plants. By switching up what they plant, gardeners can cut down on the population explosion of certain pests. If a given crop was infected by a pest or disease during one season, for example, planting a new crop in the same spot the following season might break the cycle and reduce the risk of reinfestation.
b) **Nutrient Balance**: Vegetables, fruits, and grains all have unique nutritional requirements. Crop rotation is an efficient way to prevent the depletion of certain soil nutrients because different plants draw upon and provide the soil their own distinct set of nutrients. As a result, the soil is kept in better condition and is able to retain more nutrients.
c) **Weed Management**: Some weeds are only found in specific contexts, such as in fields of a particular crop. Since weeds that have evolved to one crop may have difficulties competing with other crop types, crop rotation may be an effective way to maintain and control weed populations.
d) **Improved Soil Structure**: Better soil structure and less soil compaction can result from the wide range of root systems used by different plant species. Plants having extensive root systems, for instance, can loosen compacted soil and so increase water and air flow.
e) **Nitrogen Fixation**: Legumes (which include peas, beans, and clover) and other plants may capture atmospheric nitrogen and use it to produce nitrogen-rich compounds in the soil. A crop rotation that includes more nitrogen-fixing plants may increase soil fertility without requiring the addition of supplemental nitrogen fertilizer.

Companion Planting Benefits

The goal of companion planting is to maximize the potential for positive interactions between plants by strategically placing them in close proximity to one another.

Some of the most significant benefits of companion planting include:

a) **Pest control**: some plants release chemicals or scents that prevent pests, while others attract insects that feast on those pests. Planting compatible species creates a natural balance, deterring harmful insects while promoting beneficial ones
b) **Increased Prosperity**: Some plant combinations can boost each others growth. Certain plant combinations can promote each other's development. For instance, taller, shade-providing plants can provide shelter for sun-loving plants, and the shadow given by lower, deeper-rooted plants can help the former retain moisture.
c) **Flavor Enhancement**: Some crops may have their flavor and aroma enhanced by companion planting. The flavor may be improved as a result of this. Growing herbs like basil and mint next to your vegetables can enhance their flavor.
d) **Space Maximization**: If you have a limited amount of space for your garden, companion planting may help you maximize its potential. By interplanting crops that are compatible with one another, you may boost the overall productivity of your garden while also creating a diverse and visually beautiful setting.
e) **Soil Fertility**: Leguminous plants, called legumes, are able to fix nitrogen, which boosts soil fertility.

By including them into companion planting schemes, you can potentially boost soil quality and reap benefits for neighboring plants.

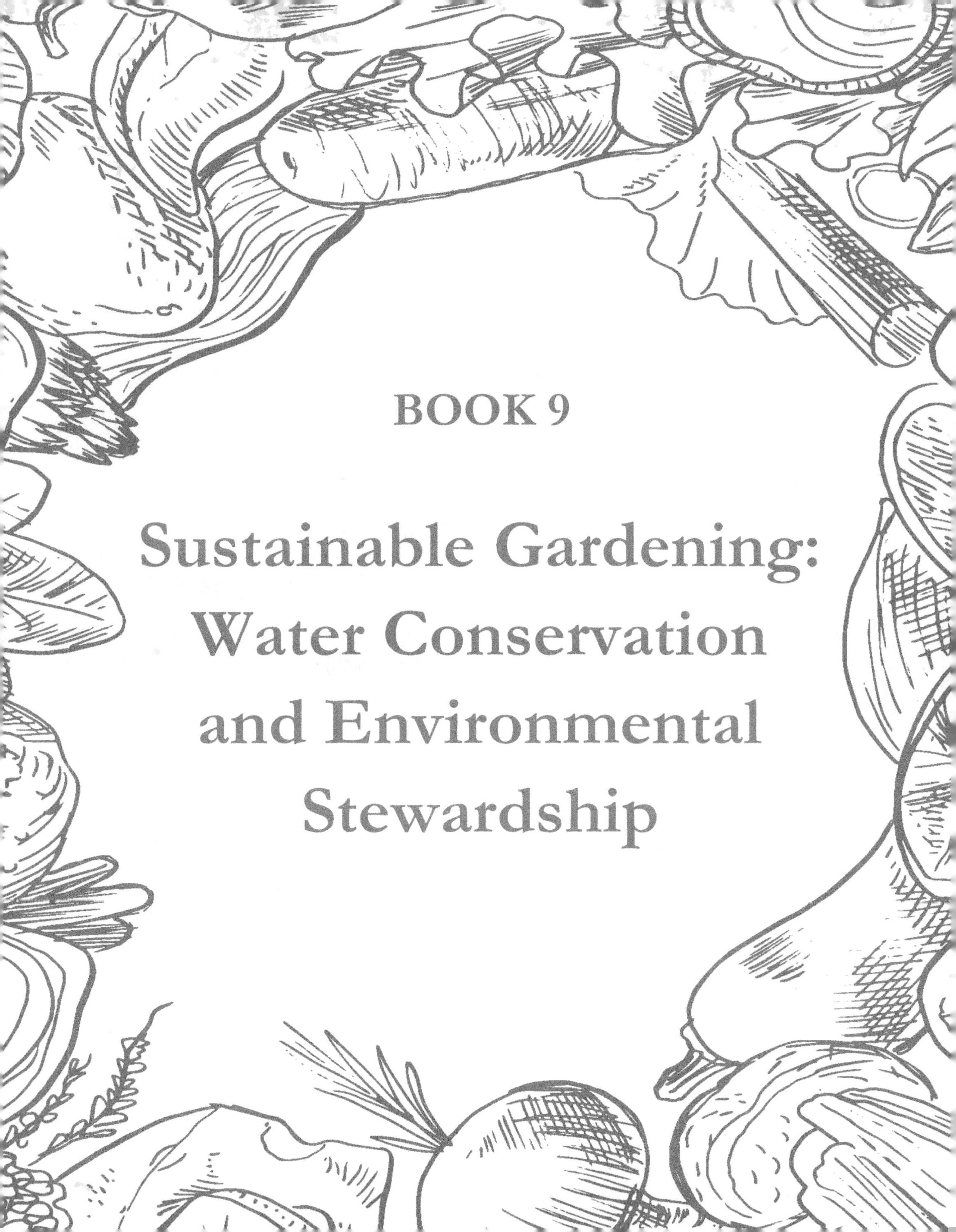

BOOK 9

Sustainable Gardening: Water Conservation and Environmental Stewardship

Book 9: Sustainable Gardening: Water Conservation and Environmental Stewardship

Introduction

Gardening that isn't harmful to the environment has become more important as a strategy for reducing the negative effects that human actions have on the world in this age of mounting environmental concerns. People are becoming increasingly aware of the significance of adopting environmentally friendly methods in all parts of their lives, including gardening, as our awareness of climate change and the destruction of the environment continues to expand. This introduction will discuss the fundamentals of sustainable gardening, with a particular emphasis on water saving and environmental stewardship as the two primary topics of discussion.

1. **Understanding Sustainable Gardening**:

   Sustainable gardening, also known as eco-friendly or ecologically responsible gardening, is a method that aims to limit the negative effect that gardening activities have on the ecosystem while simultaneously increasing biodiversity and ecological health. In other words, sustainable gardening is a kind of gardening that is environmentally responsible. It places an emphasis on the notion of judicious use of natural resources, the reduction of waste, and the maintenance of a healthy balance between the demands of humans and the preservation of the environment.

2. **Importance of Water Conservation**:

Water is a valuable resource, and as the number of people living in the world increases, it is more important than ever to make efficient use of it while preserving as much of it as possible. Traditional gardening techniques often require using an excessive amount of water, which may result in both water waste and a strain on available water supplies. A number of strategies are used in sustainable gardening to lessen the amount of water used These strategies include the utilization of drought-resistant plant species, the installation of efficient irrigation systems, and the collection of rainwater for use in the garden.

3. **Techniques for Water Conservation**:

a) Plants Capable of Withstanding Extended Periods of Drought Choosing local or adapted plants that thrive with just a little amount of irrigation is one way to dramatically cut down on the amount of water needed for a garden. These plants are able to withstand adverse situations as they adapt well to the local environment and soil conditions.
b) **Mulching**: Spreading organic mulch around plants helps to prevent weed development, minimize evaporation, and keep soil moisture. Mulch, when it decomposes, adds nutrients to the soil, which in turn encourages the development of stronger plants.
c) **Efficient Irrigation**: The installation of water-efficient irrigation systems, such as drip irrigation or soaker hoses, sends water directly to the roots of the plant, therefore reducing the amount of water that is lost to evaporation or runoff.
d) **Rainwater Harvesting**: One of the best ways to save water and lessen dependency on municipal water supply is to harvest rainwater by storing it in barrels or tanks during wetter seasons and then utilizing it to irrigate the garden during drier times.

4. **Environmental Stewardship in Gardening**:

The concept of sustainable gardening encompasses not just the reduction of water use but also a larger philosophy of environmental stewardship.

The following are some of the actions that gardeners may do to become good stewards of the environment:

a) **Composting**: Composting food scraps and yard trash not only lessens the load on landfills but also creates nutrient-dense compost that organically enhances the quality of the soil.
b) **Avoiding Chemical Pesticides**: Reducing or eliminating the use of chemical pesticides and choosing natural alternatives instead helps protect the environment from the harmful effects of toxic chemicals. This also promotes the population of beneficial insects

c) **Supporting Biodiversity**: Planting a garden with a wide range of species will increase the likelihood that beneficial insects, birds, and other forms of animals will visit your yard. This will improve the general health of the ecosystem.
d) **Reducing Waste**: Practicing responsible waste management by recycling materials, reusing containers, and reducing superfluous packaging is one way to contribute to the reduction of the garden's ecological imprint.

Watering Techniques and Strategies to Conserve Water in Gardening

Gardeners may save money by conserving water, which is not only an ecologically good practice but also useful to their financial situation. It is feasible to reduce the amount of water used while still keeping a garden in a healthy and vibrant state if proper watering procedures are followed and effective approaches are used. In this lesson, we will discuss the significance of water conservation as well as several useful techniques for increasing water efficiency in gardening:

Importance of Water Conservation in Gardening:

1. **Resource Scarcity**: Water is a limited resource, and in many areas of the world, the lack of available water is a major cause for worry. The more water that is saved in the garden, the more that will be available for use in meeting other necessary demands and supporting environmental requirements.
2. **Environmental Impact**: An excessive amount of water usage may deplete local water supplies, which in turn can affect aquatic ecosystems and cause soil to erode. Gardeners make an important contribution to the protection of natural ecosystems and the maintenance of ecological harmony when they reduce their water use.
3. **Cost Savings**: The amount of water used may have a substantial influence on the monthly utility costs, particularly during dry seasons when the need for irrigation rises. Gardeners may reduce their expenses by cutting down on water use via the use of water-saving measures.

Practical Water Conservation Techniques:

1. **Drip Irrigation**: Drip irrigation is a way of watering plants that is very effective because it allows water to be delivered straight to the roots of the plant. It does this by reducing the amount of water lost to evaporation and runoff, so ensuring that plants get just the amount of water that they need. The watering schedule may be precisely controlled thanks to the timers that can be set on drip irrigation systems.

2. **Rainwater Harvesting**: Collecting rainwater is a wonderful method to save water and minimize dependency on the water supply provided by local authorities. Rainwater may be collected and stored in barrels or tanks as part of the rainwater harvesting process. Rainwater can be collected from rooftops or other surfaces. After it has been collected, the water may be used to subsequently hydrate plants during times of drought.

3. **Mulching**: The use of organic mulch around plants helps to maintain soil moisture, which in turn reduces the frequency with which plants need to be watered. The application of mulch serves as a protective covering that stops water from evaporating from the top layer of soil and suppresses the development of weeds.

4. **Proper Timing of Watering**: Watering plants in the early morning or late afternoon is excellent because it gives the plants time to absorb the water before the water is lost to evaporation in the heat of the middle of the day. It is best to avoid watering during the warmest part of the day so as to reduce the amount of water that is lost.

5. **Soil Improvement**: A healthy soil that has strong water retention capabilities may greatly cut down on the amount of water that is used. Increasing the amount of organic matter, such as compost, that is present in the soil improves its capacity to hold onto water. As a result, plants get enough hydration for an extended length of time.

6. **Grouping Plants by Water Needs**: When designing the garden, it is vital to take the plants' water requirements into mind. It is possible to achieve greater watering efficiency by clumping together plants that have comparable watering needs. Plants that need less water will not be overwatered as a result of the demands of plants that require more water that are located nearby.

7. **Watering by Hand**: Although it may take more time, watering plants by hand enables gardeners to be more accurate and target the particular regions that require water, hence minimizing total water loss.

Choosing Native and Drought-Tolerant Plants for a Sustainable Garden

Native species and drought-resistant plants are essential resources in sustainable gardening. Plants that are native to a place have evolved to thrive in its specific climate and soil, whereas drought-resistant plants can thrive with only a trickle of water. Let's talk about why it's a good idea to use drought-resistant species and native plants in your garden, how to go about selecting and caring for those plants, and the results you may expect.

Advantages of Native Plants:

1) **Climate and Soil Adaptation**: First, they are better able to thrive in the local climate and soil since they have had millions of years to adapt. Since they've already adapted to the conditions there, they require less maintenance than exotic species.
2) **Water Efficiency**: Second, they use less water than exotic species because they have adapted over time to the rain patterns in the area. They require less irrigation because, once established, they often just need a trickle or two more.
3) **Biodiversity Boost**: Thirdly, biodiversity is boosted when native plants are used in gardens because they provide food and shelter for insects, birds, and other small creatures endemic to the area. This covers the native plant and animal life as well.
4) **Natural Defenses**; Native plants have developed their own natural defenses against local pests and illnesses, reducing the need for artificial pesticides and contributing to a more sustainable and wholesome ecosystem.
5) **Soil Health**; Native plants play a crucial role in maintaining healthy soil by enhancing soil structure, nutrient cycling, and water infiltration.

Choosing Plants That Can Withstand a Drought

1) **Research Native Plant Species**; One place to start is by learning about the native plant species that are currently in your area. Local botanical gardens, horticulture societies, or government conservation agencies are all good places to learn more about native plant options. These establishments may prove to be really useful.
2) **Consider Microclimates**; Different areas of your garden may experience different amounts of sunlight, shade, and rainfall. Pick plants that do well in each of the different microclimates so that they can grow and cope with stress as best they can.
3) **Water Requirements**; Even though native plants are typically more drought-tolerant than non-natives, it is still important to consider the specific amount of water that each type of plant requires when planning your garden. Group plants together that need the same amount of water to water them more efficiently.

Native plants have a better chance of thriving in the climate and soil of their native habitat. Determine the soil's pH and fertility using a soil test, and then select plants that thrive in that specific environment.

Maintenance of Drought-Resistant Plants:

1) **Establishment Phase**; The first phase of a plant's life cycle is called the Establishment Phase, and it requires regular watering even for drought-resistant species. Once they are established, they'll be able to fend for themselves.
2) **Mulching**; To assist limit soil moisture loss, evaporation, and weed growth, mulch organic material around drought-resistant plants.
3) **Pruning and Deadheading**; Frequent pruning and deadheading can encourage healthy growth while allowing your plants to conserve resources.
4) **Add Organic Matter**; Add compost or other organic matter to the soil to increase its water-holding ability. The soil's nutrient content will improve as a result of this, too.
5) **Paying Attention to Plant Requirements**; Always pay close attention to what your plants need. You should adjust the amount of water you give them based on their signs of stress or dehydration" to make clear that it is the plants that may show these signs

Utilizing Mulching and Proper Soil Management to Reduce Water Evaporation

The sustainable gardener's armory should include effective tools like mulching and soil management for the purpose of preserving soil moisture, boosting plant health, and lowering the amount of water that is lost to evaporation. Gardeners may establish a water-efficient garden that reduces the amount of water that is wasted and promotes a flourishing ecosystem by using mulch and implementing soil management measures as part of their gardening activities. The following sections will discuss improving water retention and evaporation control, as well as the variety of mulch materials, their application methods, and the available soil management strategies

The Role of Mulch in Conserving Soil Moisture and Reducing Weed Growth:

1. **Soil Moisture Conservation**: Mulch functions as a protective covering over the soil, minimizing the soil's direct exposure to sunlight and wind, which in turn helps to conserve the soil's moisture. This barrier aids in the retention of moisture in the soil, therefore slowing the rate of evaporation and ensuring that plant roots get an adequate supply of water at all times.
2. **Weed Suppression**: Mulch may be used to create a physical barrier that blocks sunlight and prevents weed seeds from germinating, both of which are necessary for weed development. This decreases the amount of competition for water that exists between undesirable plants and desirable ones, so enabling the latter to flourish.
3. **Temperature Regulation**: Mulch helps regulate soil temperature by insulating it from severe heat or cold, which creates a more stable environment for plant roots. This makes it an important component in integrated pest management.

Different Types of Mulch Materials and Application Techniques:

1. **Organic Mulch**: Organic mulch may be made from a variety of materials, including wood chips, straw, leaves, grass clippings, and compost, among other things. As time passes, these materials decompose, which results in an increase in the amount of organic matter and nutrients in the soil.
2. **Inorganic Mulch**: Inorganic mulch, such as stones or gravel, offers long-lasting weed control and helps retain moisture. Inorganic mulch also helps prevent soil erosion. On the other hand, unlike organic mulch, it does not provide the soil with additional nutrients.
3. **Applying Mulch**: In order to spread mulch in an efficient manner, you must first clean the area of any weeds and trash. Apply a mulch layer that is between two and four inches thick In order to avoid problems linked to moisture accumulation, you should give the plant stem some space around it.

Soil Management Practices to Enhance Water Retention and Reduce Evaporation:

1. **Organic Matter Incorporation**: The structure of the soil and its ability to retain water may both be improved by the addition of organic matter, such as compost or manure that has had sufficient time to decompose. Organic matter functions similarly to a sponge by soaking up and keeping water for the benefit of plants.

2. **Soil Aeration**: Compacted soil prevents water from penetrating and stunts the development of roots. By using a garden fork or another kind of instrument designed for aeration, one can help enhance water penetration into the soil and support healthy root growth.
3. **Proper Soil Structure**: By preserving a well-balanced soil structure that has sufficient amounts of sand, silt, and clay, one may ensure a soil that is capable of retaining moisture while at the same time allowing excess water to flow away. The structure of the soil is another factor that influences the availability of nutrients to plants.
4. **Watering Practices**: Watering plants deeply but less often fosters the development of deep root systems that can reach water deeper in the soil and minimize the amount of water that is lost via evaporation at the soil surface.
5. **Mulching with Organic Matter**: As mentioned earlier, as organic material decomposes, it contributes beneficial nutrients to the soil

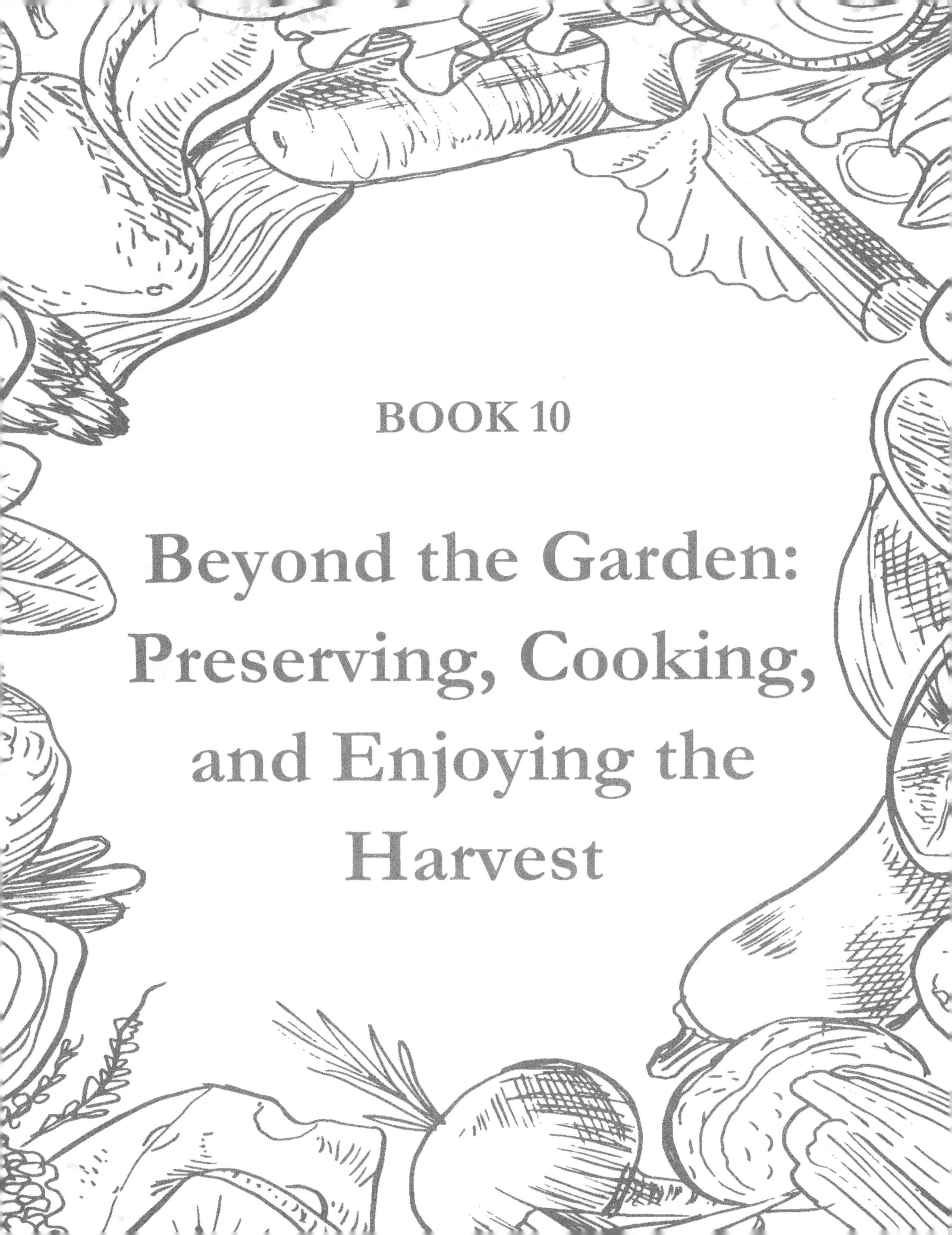

BOOK 10

Beyond the Garden: Preserving, Cooking, and Enjoying the Harvest

Book 10: Beyond the Garden: Preserving, Cooking, and Enjoying the Harvest

Introduction

Hello. Welcome to the world of canning, cooking and appreciating the fruits of your labor! This book aims to guide you in exploring the art of preserving and preparing foods. Whether you have a garden, love visiting farmers' markets, or simply want to make the most of produce this guide is for you.

Preserving for Abundant Harvests

When the harvest season is abundant, it's common to find yourself with an excess of fruits, vegetables and herbs. That's where preserving comes in handy. By extending the shelf life of these ingredients through methods like freezing, canning, drying, pickling or fermenting; you can enjoy them throughout the year. In this book we'll delve into each preservation technique and help you determine which one suits types of food best—each method has its unique advantages and flavors.

Canning

Canning is a method, for preserving fruits and vegetables that continues to grow in popularity. One way to prevent food from spoiling is, by sterilizing the produce and then storing it in heat treated jars that are properly sealed. Canned products can last for months or even years making them a great option for long term storage.

Freezing

Another method to maintain the freshness of harvested food without using chemicals or extensive preparation is freezing. Fruits, vegetables and herbs can be frozen and used in various ways throughout the year.

Drying.

Drying is a technique for preserving food by removing moisture from fruits, vegetables and herbs. The resulting concentrated flavors can be used in recipes.

Pickling and Fermentation

Pickling involves pouring a brine or vinegar solution over vegetables or fruits and submerging them during the pickling process. Fermentation is another natural preservation technique that utilizes bacteria to transform ingredients into delicious, probiotic-rich meals. This process not only preserves the produce but also adds acidic and savory flavors. Not only are fermented foods tasty, they also offer great benefits for your digestive system

Enhancing the Flavor and Complexity of Your Cooking with Preserved Ingredients

Preserved ingredients bring depth and complexity to the dishes you create in your kitchen. Just imagine the burst of flavors that come from using your homemade tomato sauce in winter pasta dishes or incorporating pickled vegetables into light and refreshing summer salads. By cooking with preserved ingredients, you can enjoy the taste of produce all year round and have the freedom to explore various recipes.

Preserving the Harvest: Methods and Techniques

Canning.

Preserving food, in airtight jars using the technique of canning is a method to keep fruits and vegetables fresh for longer. The process involves heating the food to eliminate any bacteria and creating a vacuum seal to prevent spoilage. There are two approaches to canning;

a) **Water Bath Canning**; This method is suitable for preserving goods with acid content, such as pickles, tomatoes and fruits. After preparing the food it is placed in jars covered with a liquid (a sugar or vinegar based solution) and immersed in a water bath at the temperature for the required duration.

b) **Pressure Canning**; To preserve low acid goods like vegetables, meats and soups safely pressure canning becomes necessary. This technique involves subjecting the items to higher temperatures than water bath canning for food safety To perform pressure canning you will need a canner designed to handle these pressures.

Pickling

Pickling is not only a way to preserve vegetables and fruits but also an opportunity to infuse them with new and exciting flavors. In this method you can brine the product by submerging it in a solution made of water, vinegar, salt and various spices. This fermentation process adds an distinct flavor, to the pickles. Feel free to experiment with seasonings to create a range of pickles, such as bread and butter, dill, spicy or sweet varieties.

Jams and Jellies

Making jams and jellies is a way to preserve the sweetness of fruits. All you need to do is cook the fruit with sugar and sometimes pectin (a gelling ingredient found in fruits). Once done pour the mixture into sterilized jars. Seal them tightly. Jellies have an transparent texture while jams have a chunky consistency, with fruit fragments.

Freezing:

Freezing is a versatile preservation technique that helps maintain the flavors and nutrients of fruits and vegetables. To freeze produce properly;

1. Choose high quality produce.
2. Clean the vegetables thoroughly. Blanch them before freezing to deactivate enzymes that can lead to spoilage.
3. Use sealed containers or freezer bags to prevent freezer burn.
4. Make sure to label and date the packages, for identification.

Drying

Drying fruits, vegetables, and herbs is a preservation method that has been used by humans for a long time. By removing moisture from the produce you can prevent the growth of molds and bacteria which helps extend the shelf life of the food. There are ways to dry foods including;

a) **Sun Drying**; This traditional method involves exposing food to sunlight so it can naturally dry out. However it works best in dry climates. May not be suitable for all locations.

b) **Oven Drying**; While its possible to dry fruits and herbs in an oven at temperatures this method may not be the energy efficient choice.
c) **Dehydrator**; An electric food dehydrator offers an efficient way to dry a range of foods while ensuring consistent drying without exposure, to contaminants.

With some effort, you can easily become skilled in preserving food, and each method offers unique flavors and textures.

Recipes and Cooking Tips for Using Homegrown Vegetables

Whether you have a flourishing garden or access to freshly produced local vegetables, there are an infinite number of ways to showcase the flavors and appreciate the inherent freshness of those vegetables. Here are some delicious recipes and helpful cooking advice to make the most of your harvest:

1. Grilled Vegetable Salad

This recipe makes 4 servings

Ingredients:

- Assorted vegetables from your garden (zucchini, bell peppers, cherry tomatoes, eggplants, and onions)
- Olive oil
- Balsamic vinegar
- Salt and pepper
- Optional: Fresh basil leaves

Instructions:

1. Wash and cut the vegetables into bite-sized pieces.
2. Preheat the grill to medium-high heat.
3. Brush the vegetables with olive oil, ensuring they are evenly coated.
4. Place the oiled vegetables on the grill and cook until they are tender with a slight char. Turn them occasionally to ensure even cooking.
5. The approximate cooking times for different vegetables are as follows:
    - **Zucchini**: 3-4 minutes per side
    - **Bell peppers**: 5-7 minutes per side
    - **Cherry tomatoes**: 2-3 minutes (can be skewered or placed in a grill basket)
    - **Eggplants**: 4-5 minutes per side
    - **Onions**: 4-5 minutes per side
6. Once grilled to perfection, remove the vegetables from the grill and transfer them to a large bowl.
7. Drizzle balsamic vinegar over the grilled vegetables, and season with salt and pepper according to your taste preference.
8. If desired, tear some fresh basil leaves and add them to the salad for an extra burst of flavor and aroma.
9. Toss all the ingredients together gently until the vegetables are evenly coated with the dressing.
10. Divide the grilled vegetable salad into four equal portions.

Nutritional Value (per serving):

- Calories: approximately 120-150 kcal (depending on the amount and type of vegetables used)
- Fat: 7-10g (mostly from olive oil)
- Fiber: 5-8g
- Vitamins: High levels of Vitamin A, Vitamin C, and Vitamin K
- Minerals: Rich in potassium and magnesium

---

2. Stuffed Bell Peppers

This recipe makes 4 stuffed bell peppers

Ingredients:

- 4 large grown bell peppers (any color of your choice)
- 1 cup quinoa or brown rice
- 1 pound lean ground turkey or firm tofu (for an alternative)
- 1 small onion, finely chopped
- 2 garlic cloves, minced
- 1 cup tomato sauce
- Optional: 1/2 cup shredded cheese (cheddar, mozzarella, or your favorite type)
- Salt and pepper to taste
- Italian herbs (oregano, basil, thyme) to taste

Instructions:

1. Preheat your oven to 375°F (190°C).
2. Cut off the tops of the bell peppers and remove the seeds and membranes. Rinse them thoroughly.
3. Prepare the quinoa or brown rice following the instructions on the package and set it aside.
4. In a skillet over medium heat, cook the ground turkey or tofu along with chopped onion and

garlic until it's nicely browned and cooked through. Season with salt, pepper, and Italian herbs to your taste.

5. In a large mixing bowl, combine the cooked meat/tofu with the cooked quinoa/rice and tomato sauce. Mix everything well until it's evenly combined and coated in the sauce.
6. Stuff each bell pepper with the mixture, pressing it down gently to ensure they are tightly packed.
7. If desired, sprinkle shredded cheese on top of each stuffed pepper.
8. Place the stuffed bell peppers in a baking dish. Cover the dish with foil.
9. Bake in the preheated oven for around 25-30 minutes until the peppers become tender.

Nutritional Information (per stuffed bell pepper):

- Calories: Approximately 300-350 kcal (depending on the ingredients used)
- Protein: 25-30g (if using turkey) / 15-20g (if using tofu)
- Carbohydrates: 30-35g
- Fiber: 5-7g
- Fat: 10-12g (if using turkey) / 7-8g (if using tofu)
- Vitamins: Rich in Vitamin A and Vitamin C

---

3. Fresh Tomato and Basil Pasta

This recipe makes 2-3 servings

Ingredients:

- Homegrown tomatoes
- Fresh basil leaves
- 8 ounces (225g) wheat spaghetti or any pasta of your preference
- 3 tablespoons olive oil
- 2 garlic cloves, minced
- Salt and pepper to taste
- Optional: Grated Parmesan cheese

Instructions:

1. Cook the pasta according to the instructions on the package until it reaches al dente perfection. Drain the cooked pasta and set it aside.
2. While the pasta is cooking, dice the tomatoes and finely chop the basil leaves.
3. In a pan, heat the olive oil over medium heat. Gently sauté the minced garlic until it becomes aromatic and slightly golden.
4. Add the diced tomatoes to the pan and cook them until their juices start to release and the tomatoes soften slightly.
5. Season the tomato mixture with salt and pepper to taste. Stir in the chopped basil leaves for added flavor and aroma.
6. Toss the cooked pasta in the tomato basil sauce until it is well coated.
7. If desired, sprinkle grated Parmesan cheese on top before serving for an extra burst of flavor.

Nutritional Information (per serving):

- Calories: Approximately 350-400 kcal (depending on the type of pasta used and amount of cheese added)
- Protein: 8-10g (depending on the type of pasta used)
- Carbohydrates: 50-60g (depending on the type of pasta used)
- Fiber: 8-10g (if using whole wheat pasta)
- Fat: 12-15g (mostly from olive oil and cheese)
- Vitamins: High in Vitamin A and Vitamin C
- Antioxidant: Contains lycopene from tomatoes
- Healthy Fats: Contains healthy fats from olive oil

---

4. Garden Vegetable Stir Fry

This recipe makes 2-3 servings

Ingredients:

- 1 cup harvested broccoli florets
- 1 cup julienne-cut carrots
- 1 cup snap peas
- 1 cup sliced bell peppers (any color of your choice)
- 1/2 cup chopped onions
- 2 cloves minced garlic
- 1 teaspoon grated ginger
- 3 tablespoons soy sauce or tamari (for gluten-free option)
- 2 tablespoons sesame oil
- Optional: Sesame seeds for garnish

- Cooked brown rice or quinoa (for serving)

Instructions:

1. In a wok or large skillet, heat sesame oil over medium-high heat.
2. Add minced garlic and grated ginger to the wok. Sauté for about a minute until they become fragrant.
3. Add the chopped onions, sliced bell peppers, julienne-cut carrots, snap peas, and harvested broccoli florets to the wok. Stir-fry the vegetables for a few minutes until they reach a tender-crisp texture. Avoid overcooking to retain their nutrients and vibrant colors.
4. Drizzle soy sauce or tamari over the stir-fried vegetables. Toss gently to ensure that the sauce coats all the vegetables evenly.
5. Remove the wok from heat.

Optional: Sprinkle some sesame seeds on top for added crunch and flavor.

1. Serve the Garden Vegetable Stir Fry over cooked brown rice or quinoa as a nutritious base.

Nutritional Information (excluding rice/quinoa and optional sesame seeds):

- Calories: Approximately 150-200 kcal (depending on the amount of oil used)
- Protein: 6-8g
- Carbohydrates: 15-20g
- Fiber: 5-7g
- Fat: 8-10g (mostly from sesame oil)
- Vitamins: High in Vitamin A, Vitamin C, and Vitamin K
- Minerals: Rich in potassium and manganese

---

5. Roasted Root Vegetables

This recipe makes 4 servings

Ingredients:

- 2 cups harvested carrots, peeled and cut into sticks
- 2 cups harvested beets, peeled and diced
- 2 cups freshly harvested sweet potatoes, peeled and diced
- 3 tablespoons olive oil
- Fresh rosemary or thyme (or dried herbs as an alternative)
- Salt and pepper to taste

Instructions:

1. Preheat your oven to 400°F (200°C).
2. In a large bowl, toss the diced carrots, beets, and sweet potatoes with olive oil until they are well coated.
3. Season the vegetable mixture with fresh rosemary or thyme (or dried herbs, if using), salt, and pepper. Toss again to ensure even distribution of the seasonings.
4. Spread out the seasoned vegetables in a single layer on a baking sheet lined with parchment paper.
5. Place the baking sheet with the medley of root vegetables in the preheated oven. Let them roast for 25-30 minutes, keeping an eye on them until they reach a tender and slightly caramelized state. The roasting time may vary depending on the size of the vegetable pieces, so adjust accordingly.

Nutritional Information:

- Calories: Approximately 150-200 kcal (depending on the amount of oil used)
- Protein: 3-5g
- Carbohydrates: 25-30g
- Fiber: 5-7g
- Fat: 7-10g (mostly from olive oil)
- Vitamins: High in Vitamin A and Vitamin C
- Minerals: Rich in potassium and iron

Cooking Advice:

- Gather veggies right before using them for optimal flavor.
- Keep preparations simple to fully appreciate the fresh flavors.
- Experiment with grilling, roasting, sautéing, or steaming vegetables to explore different flavors and textures.
- Combine various vegetables to create tasty and healthy meals.
- Enhance the flavors of your homegrown vegetables with fresh herbs and spices.

By using these tips and recipes, you can elevate the flavors of your homegrown vegetables and savor the delicious fruits of your labor in the garden. Embrace simple, locally sourced ingredients to cook memorable meals that capture the essence of each harvest. Enjoy your flavorful and nourishing creations!

Exploring Different Culinary Traditions and Flavors from Around the World

One way to broaden your horizons and make your vegetable based meals more exciting is by embarking on an adventure to explore the tastes and cooking traditions of different countries around the world. Each region has its culinary traditions, so incorporating ingredients and cooking styles from other cultures can elevate the flavors of your fresh veggies. Let's explore some cuisines known for their tastes;

Mediterranean Cuisine; The Mediterranean region is renowned for its focus on fresh ingredients. To infuse a touch of the Mediterranean into your vegetable dishes try using flavors like olive oil, garlic, lemon oregano and basil. Roasting vegetables with a drizzle of olive oil and a sprinkle of Mediterranean herbs showcases this heritage beautifully.

Asian Cuisine; Asian cuisine offers a range of flavors from the Thai curries to the flavorful umami of Japanese miso. To create stir fries noodle dishes and curries with an Asian influence, you can experiment with a variety of ingredients, like soy sauce, ginger, lemongrass, coconut milk and sesame oil. When it comes to Indian cuisine, the flavors are rich and vibrant due to the array of spices used. Ingredients such as garam masala, turmeric, cumin, coriander and cardamom can greatly enhance the taste of rice based dishes, lentil recipes and vegetable curries.

Middle Eastern Cuisine; Middle Eastern cuisine is known for its flavors and textural variations. To infuse your salads with Middle Eastern flair or add some zest to veggies and dips consider incorporating ingredients like tahini paste sumac spice blend, pomegranate molasses for a touch, or za'atar seasoning mix If you crave the flavors of Mexican cuisine on your plate don't forget to include chili peppers for a kick of heat along with fresh cilantro leaves for added freshness. Squeeze in some lime juice to brighten up your dishes and elevate them further by incorporating avocados. Try creating mouthwatering tacos filled with vegetables or savor flavorful fajitas and enchiladas, seasoned with spices.

Italian Cuisine; Italian cooking lies in its simplicity and the ability to let the quality of ingredients shine. To enhance vegetable based meals try incorporating tomato-based sauces, herbs like basil and oregano. Finish them off with a sprinkle of grated Parmesan or Pecorino cheese for added flavor.

Caribbean Cuisine; Caribbean cuisine offers a blend of flavors influenced by Africa, Europe and Asia. Known for its deliciousness Caribbean cuisine can be enjoyed by preparing vegetable stews and sides infused with Jamaican inspired seasonings like coconut milk, jerk seasoning, allspice and Scotch bonnet peppers.

Thai Cuisine; Thai cuisine is renowned for its balance of spicy, sour, sweet, and salty flavors. To infuse your dishes with a taste of Thailand incorporate Thai ingredients such as fish sauce, lime juice, Thai basil and chili peppers.

Embrace the opportunity to experiment and combine flavors from different cuisines as you explore the various approaches to food preparation available. Why not try adding a touch of the Mediterranean to lentils influenced by India or incorporating spices, from Thailand into a Middle Eastern inspired vegetable dish? The possibilities are endless. Exploring flavors from around the world will bring an adventurous and exciting element to your cooking.

Consider experimenting with dishes from cultures and putting your spin on them, using the vegetables you've grown in your garden. This will enhance your experience. Embrace the range of tastes, cooking techniques and ingredients found globally allowing your vegetable-based meals to transport you to far-off places through the sensory experience of taste. Let yourself get excited about the fusion of flavors from around the world and enjoy the pleasure of cooking with the abundance from your garden.

Exploring Diverse Cuisines and Traditional Recipes with Homegrown Vegetables

Growing your vegetables opens up a world of possibilities allowing you to explore unique and delicious recipes from various culinary traditions. Let's take a journey and discover some recipes that showcase the abundance of your garden;

1. **Ratatouille (French Cuisine)**; Ratatouille is a vegetable stew originating from the Provencal region of France. It beautifully captures the flavors of vegetables, like eggplant, zucchini, bell peppers, tomatoes and onions. These vibrant ingredients are cooked with spices and herbs such as thyme and rosemary. Whether served as a side dish or a main course, hot or cold this rich and colorful meal is a way to savor the essence of your garden produce.

2. **Greek Spanakopita (Greek Cuisine)**; Indulge in the mouthwatering delights of Greek cuisine, with Spanakopita – a dish made by wrapping spinach and feta cheese in flaky phyllo dough. The taste and freshness of this recipe reach heights when you use spinach from your garden. The delightful combination of spinach and tangy feta cheese creates an delightful treat that can be enjoyed as a snack, appetizer or even a light dinner.

3. **Indian Vegetable Biryani (Indian Cuisine)**; Biryani is a savory rice dish that showcases the array of Indian spices. You can customize this dish to your liking by incorporating vegetables, like carrots, peas, potatoes and cauliflower. To make it a flavorful and satisfying lunch option infuse the dish with spices such as cumin, cardamom, cinnamon and saffron. This will ensure that the aroma of the dish tantalizes your senses.

4. **Caprese Salad (Italian Cuisine)**; The Caprese salad is an Italian creation that exemplifies the use of simple yet fresh ingredients. Arrange slices of garden tomatoes, with cubes of mozzarella cheese and fragrant basil leaves; then drizzle with virgin olive oil and a touch of balsamic glaze. During the summer months this salad serves as an appetizer or side dish because it highlights the inherent qualities of these vegetables in their purest form.

5. **Japanese Vegetable Tempura (Japanese Cuisine)**; Tempura is a dish in Japanese cuisine where vegetables are delicately coated with batter and then deep fried. To enjoy an crispy tempura you can use zucchini, sweet potatoes, bell peppers and mushrooms. For a burst of flavors serve it with tentsuyu, which is a dipping sauce.

6. **Stuffed Bell Peppers (Mexican Cuisine:** Take advantage of the colors of bell peppers by incorporating them into a Mexican inspired dish. Create a filling using rice, black beans, corn, chopped tomatoes along with spices like cumin and chili powder. Stuff the peppers with this mixture. Bake them until the peppers turn tender and the filling becomes bubbly. Add cheese as a topping before baking.

7. **Lebanese Tabbouleh (Middle Eastern Cuisine)**; Tabbouleh is a salad that originates from Lebanon and is part of Middle Eastern cuisine. It consists of bulgur wheat mixed with parsley and mint leaves along, with tomatoes, cucumbers and lemon juice.

The taste of this flavorful salad becomes more delightful when you cultivate your own herbs and vegetables. It adds a healthy touch to any meal.

8. **Thai Green Curry (Thai Cuisine)**; Prepare a Thai curry using homegrown vegetables like eggplant, bamboo shoots, green beans and bell peppers. This dish originates from Thailand. To truly experience Thai cuisine gently simmer the chicken and veggies in a green curry sauce made with coconut milk, Thai green curry paste, and aromatic herbs such as lemongrass and kaffir lime leaves.

Other Helpful Gardening Tips

- **Effective Weed Control Tips**
  - If you were to start tracking your time spent in the garden, you would realize one thing. You probably spend a lot of time on weeding. The first few hours of weeding are somewhat satisfying for new gardeners, but it gets boring pretty quickly. Luckily, there are ways to contain their growth so that your plants get as much nutrients as they need.
  - Some say that a garden needs weeds. While it is true that weeds are nature's way of healing an area without a plant, weeds and gardeners have very different ideas for what constitutes a good recovery. With a better understanding of weeds as well as the strategies we will go over in this section, you can give yourself an edge over these green pests and more time to enjoy your beautiful garden.

- **Weeds are Timebombs**
  - Think of it this way: weed seeds are everywhere. Every square inch of your garden has them However, they only grow if they get enough light. When that happens, germination is triggered and weeds start to grow. How do you utilize this information?
  - Simple. The act of digging and cultivating disturbs the soil, which may bring the seeds to the surface. So, always assume that the weed seeds are there, ready to burst every time you move any soil. To minimize weed growth, only dig where you need to and immediately cover the disturbed area with plants or mulch.
  - What do you do when you need to remove dandelions? Take a sharp knife with a narrow blade and slice through the roots and other lawn weeds. That way, you sever their food source and they will wilt away so you do not have to uproot them and risk having a weed outbreak. Never underestimate weed. Their seeds can remain dormant for a long time.

- **Mulch**
  - Sometimes, you just have to disturb the soil, especially during the planting process. This brings up weed seeds to the surface. But remember that they still need light before they can grow, so do not give them the chance to see sunlight. Use mulch to cover up, be it wood chips, bark nuggets, pine needles, straw, etc. Mulch will deteriorate away, so make sure to replace them to keep weeds at bay.
  - Mulch is going to be your best friend when you get into gardening. Not only does it keep weeds down, but they also keep the soil nice and moist for your plant. If you go with organic mulches, they will make great homes for crickets and carabid beetles. These are your friends since they seek out and devour weed seeds for you.
  - Keep in mind that chunky mulches might allow some light through. You might discover a little too late that the mulch you used actually has weed seeds. What do you do then? Throw in more mulch. Make sure to replenish it as needed. You know you have enough when there are 2 inches of the stuff. Too much mulch can deprive the soil of oxygen, which might kill off your seeds." since you're likely referring to more than one seed., you can just throw cardboard, newspaper, or biodegradable fabric over the surface and then put more mulch over it.

- What if you plan to use this method on areas that you hardly touch, such as the root zones of trees or shrubs. In this case, start with a layer of tough landscape fabric. The idea is to block out light first. You can then throw in mulch. Keep in mind that weed seeds can also be carried by the wind or by birds. So, when there is enough organic matter on the sheet, weeds can start to grow. For the sheet to be effective, you need to uproot the weed before they penetrate the fabric and into the ground.

- **Weed when Weeding is Good**
  - The best time to uproot some weeds is after a good rain. Put on a pair of gloves, a sitting pad, and a tarp and go ham on the weeds. Do not forget to take an old table fork so you can work out the tendrils of chickweed or henbit. If you go after something like taprooted weeds like a dock or a dandelion, consider using a fishtail weeder. The reason why you need to do it after a rain is simple. The soil is nice and wet, so it is very pliable. The soil will give way to a bit of force and you can pull out the weeds – root and stem.
  - But you do not have to wait until the rain comes. If you need to take care of weeds now, you just need to slice off below the soil with a hoe or a similar tool. The idea is to sever the weeds from their roots and they will promptly shrivel off and perish. If you use mulch, take an old steak knife and slice off the weeds from their roots, and then patch up any open spaces.

- **Composting Weeds**
  - Weeds do have a use, so do not just throw them away. They make excellent compost, but you cannot just chuck it into the compost bin either. You see, most weeds already contain seeds and nobody has the time nor patience to deseed weeds. It is just impractical. Fortunately, seeds will die off when it gets hot enough.
  - Keeping your compost nice and warm requires precise mixing and remixing of materials. Heating everything up will be troublesome, so wait until they almost reach that rotted state before you start.
  - From there, just solarize small batches of moist compost by storing it in black plastic nursery liners enclosed in clear plastic bags. Allow them to bask in the sun for a couple of days.
  - However, keep in mind that heat does a lot more than just killing weed seeds. It also destroys most of the microscopic lifeforms that give compost its effectiveness. Therefore, you want to reprocess cooked compost at least a few weeks before you actually use it in your garden. Throw your compost into a plastic storage bin alongside a handful of earthworms and let them do their work. Soon, it will be full of humic acids and other compounds that make your compost great again.

- **Delay Through Decapitation**
  - Sometimes, maybe because of time constraints, you cannot uproot weeds. Ideally, you want to uproot weeds, but if you do not have that option, you can just chop off their heads. Of course, the roots and stems are still there, so it is not a permanent solution. However, beheading will give you a few weeks of time before the weed grows back and start spreading its seeds everywhere. Plus, you force the weed to allocate resources to regrow their lost parts, therefore exhausting their food supply and root buds, which also slow their spread.

- For towers of ragweed or poke, you need pruning loppers. Alternatively, you can use a string trimmer with a blade attachment to nip off prickly thistles or brambles down. Regardless, when you lop off their heads, weeds will focus on recovery first before reproduction.

- **Mind the Gaps**
  - You should never plant your crops too close to each other since they will get in each other's way. However, try to plant them just close enough so that they choke out emerging weeds with their shades. By planning out your garden, you can limit the number of weed-friendly gaps from the start by planting your plants close together. This little trick alone can reduce the weed population by at least 25 percent.
  - So, how far away should your plants be from each other? Spacing recommendations are based on the assumption that your plants will just touch each other when they mature. You can find guidelines for plants that are especially prone to foliar diseases and other guides about spacing for your particular plant online.

- **Water the Plants, Not the Weeds**
  - Similar to plants, weeds also require water to survive. You can make use of drought by depriving weeds of water. How? You can use drip or soaker hoses that go underneath mulch to keep your plants nicely hydrated while keeping the weeds nearby parched. If done correctly, this can effectively remove weed-seed germination by up to 70 percent.
  - However, you still need to watch out for deeply rooted perennial weeds such as nutsedge and bindweed in moist areas. They can rapidly increase with the benefits of drip irrigation.
  - On top of these strategies, you should always use organic matter to enrich your soil as that helps reduce weed growth as well. Scientists are still scratching their heads over this one but the results are clear. Fewer weed seeds germinate in soil that is rich in compost and organic matter.
  - As mentioned before, weeds grow where other plants usually cannot. This is mother nature's way of healing. She populates nutrition-sparse soil with weeds so that they may make the soil friendlier for other plants in the future. One working theory here is that when the soil is healthy and full of nutrients, there is no need for weeds to grow. They are not meant to grow on fertile soil, so they are less likely to appear.

- **Understanding Frost Dates**
  - Timing is everything. If you plant too early or too late in the season and your garden might spectacularly fail. Find out what the last average spring frost date is in your area. That way, you know when it is safe to start planting. Putting out your seeds prematurely would just kill them off anyway.
  - While you are at it, find out what the first average fall frost date is as well. It tells you when you should harvest your plants, or at least move them indoors before the cold could do any harm to them.

- **Know Your USDA Hardiness Zone**
    - Think of it as a guide to help you know which plants won't survive the winter in your area. Moreover, you will also have a better idea of when you should expect your last frost date in spring so that you know when to start planting veggies, fruits, and other annuals outside.

- **Pruning**
    - Here are some helpful tips on when to prune. For spring-flowering shrubs like lilacs and large flower climbing roses, go for it immediately after the blooms fade. Those plants set their flower buds in fall/autumn on last year's growth. If you prune them in winter or fall, you also remove next spring's flower buds.

- **Site It Right**
    - Location is pretty much everything, just like real estate. As mentioned before, it should get plenty of sunlight. More importantly, however, make sure it is in a location where you see it regularly.

- **Look at the Sun**
    - One common mistake newbie gardeners make is misjudging sunlight. Spend a couple of days noting where the sunlight travels throughout the day. Your garden should be on that path, ideally receiving as much sunlight as possible. If you raise your plants in containers, you may even need to move them around in the morning and evening from one window to another. How much time should your plants spend sunbathing? Most edible plants require 6 hours a day, so that is the minimum exposure you need to aim for.

- **Water**
    - Logistics is also important. Your garden should be near a water source. Indoor gardens should be easy to figure out, so this tip applies to those who have more real estate in their backyard. Make sure that your hose can reach all of your plants. While hauling buckets of water makes for an effective workout, it gets old quickly.

- **Start with the Soil**
    - Your plants rely on the soil for almost everything, so it makes sense that investing in the soil itself would lead to great results. If you lack real estate, you can always grow your plants in containers. Make sure the containers are big enough for the plant it is housing and fill them with a high-quality potting mix. These mixes help plants in pots thrive and some even prevent over- and under-watering.

- **Picking the Right Plants**
    - Every plant is different, so make sure to match them to your growing conditions. So, sun-loving plants should be in a spot where they get to see a lot of sunlight whereas heat-tolerant plants can be planted in warmer climates. Ground-gobbling vines such as melons and pumpkins need enough elbow rooms or trellis to climb.

    - It all comes down to understanding the plants you want to grow. The internet should contain all the information you need to ensure that your plant has the best possible conditions to thrive.

- **Use Manure Wisely**
    - When it comes to manure, only use compost, rotted manure that has cured for at least 6 months before you chuck it on your soil. Fresh manure has too much nitrogen and it can "burn" your plants. Plus, it might also contain parasites and pathogens, and you want neither of them anywhere near your plants. Manure from dogs, cats, and pigs has no place in the gardens or compost piles since they may contain parasites that infect humans.

- **Growing Season**
    - Understanding how much time you have for your growing season is crucial. That way, you know whether you have enough time to get a plant going before having to move them indoors or just wait until the winter is over.

Conclusion

he G.R.O.W. System has proven to be an effective approach for growing vegetables It serves as the theme that connects the takeaways and highlights from each book in this comprehensive resource. This system, which originated from a group of gardeners in the United Kingdom is represented by the acronym G.R.O.W. standing for "Gather, Research, Organize and Work." Through our exploration of gardening methods and practices we consistently observed how utilizing the G.R.O.W. System can significantly enhance success and satisfaction in gardening endeavors.

As readers we are now inspired to embark on our vegetable farming journey with confidence. Armed with the knowledge and insights gained from these books we can approach gardening with increased assurance and enthusiasm. The G.R.O.W. System acts as a guiding principle that offers an practical approach to navigating the complex world of vegetable gardening. It makes this world more accessible not to beginners but, to seasoned gardeners who wish to further improve their skills.

To ensure that readers fully grasp the value provided by this gardening resource and guide it's crucial to emphasize its significance. By incorporating the G.R.O.W. System into our gardening practices we gain a strategy to tackle any challenges that may arise on our land. This system encompasses a wealth of knowledge, useful tips and effective strategies applicable, to all stages of cultivation. From planning and preparation to nurturing and harvesting the plants as they mature.

Lets also take a moment to appreciate the joy that comes with cultivating our vegetables. Gardening offers us an opportunity to connect with nature and our surroundings experience the satisfaction of growing vegetables for ourselves and loved ones and witness the transformation from tiny seeds into thriving plants. Despite setbacks along the way the overall experience of nurturing life and marveling at natures wonders is truly unparalleled.

In conclusion it is evident that the G.R.O.W System represents a groundbreaking approach, to vegetable farming. With a sense of assurance we can embark on our gardening journey, armed with a resource and guide to support us at each stage. We have thoroughly familiarized ourselves with the insights and noteworthy aspects, from each book. Let's revel in the joy of gardening and relish the rewards that arise from participating in this gratifying pursuit. Here's, to a gardening experience!

SUPPLEMENTARY CONTENTS

Unlock Hidden Garden Treasures!

Scan the QR code below to access three exclusive enhancements that perfectly complement your journey in "Vegetable Gardener's Mastery." These hidden gems offer valuable insights, thought-provoking reflections, and hands-on exercises to enrich your gardening experience and take your sustainable practices to new heights. Embrace this enriching opportunity and continue uncovering the layers of wisdom within the pages of this book. Let the journey to a flourishing garden unfold!

If you encounter any issues or have feedback to share, feel free to reach out directly to the Mindsparkpress LTD Facebook page. Your input is invaluable in our mission to provide the best possible support to our readers. Let the revelations begin!

YOUR FEEDBACK MATTERS

Dear Reader,

Thank you for joining me on this transformative journey of "Vegetable Gardener's Mastery." I trust that this book has opened up new horizons in your understanding of sustainable gardening and cultivating a harmonious connection with nature.

If you found the information in this book valuable and insightful for your journey in gardening, **I kindly ask for a moment of your time to consider leaving an honest review on Amazon**. Your feedback is invaluable, and it will help fellow readers discover the enriching world of mindful gardening and eco-conscious practices.

By sharing your thoughts and experiences, you not only support this book but also play a significant role in inspiring others to embrace a more sustainable and fulfilling gardening approach. Your words can be a guiding light for those seeking to cultivate a deeper connection with the earth and foster a vibrant garden.

Should you have any suggestions, questions, or insights you'd like to share, please don't hesitate to reach out to us through our Facebook pages, "Mindsparkpress LTD" or "Benjamin Greenfield." Your contribution will aid us in refining future editions and ensuring that this book continues to offer the best possible assistance to its readers.

Once again, thank you for being part of this journey. Together, let us continue to embrace the transformative power of mindful gardening and cultivate a thriving, sustainable future.

With heartfelt gratitude,

Benjamin Greenfield

Made in the USA
Las Vegas, NV
17 February 2025

18306460R00079